ORGY IN ANOTHER WORLD

Kio watched it all with the disgust only a once-civilized man could know. He passed back into the crowd in the Great Hut, pausing briefly over the one-eyed twins, Mishla and Cular. Kio let his eyes roam, hoping they'd settle on the woman who shadowed him, so he did not see the way the two young warriors occupied themselves with another set of twins—a pair of hermaphrodites dressed and painted half as women, half as men. Mishla and Cular worked over these dual natures with spitting fury.

Between bouts, the archers sent their feathered shafts into the air and the smoky clouds rained down the bodies of white doves.

In another corner of the hut, Careem, his stump bared and twitching like the head of a seal, toyed with his own special pet. It was a black Watut without arms or legs who squirmed along the dirt floor like a grub.

THE AMAZONS
OF
SOMELON

Raymond Kaminski

LEISURE BOOKS ❧ **NEW YORK CITY**

A LEISURE BOOK

Published by

Nordon Publications, Inc.
Two Park Avenue
New York, N.Y. 10016

Chapter 1

Caravan

Tolling like a bell lost in the ruins of some pagan cathedral, the wind drifted in off the desert. It had raged unopposed over the dunes, freezing the life out of salamanders and vipers. Now it wriggled through rock-studded hills, searching for more challenging, warm-blooded prey in the moonlight. At the mouth of the canyon, the wind grazed a line of Teutite wagons creeking blindly over the rutted road, and there it curled, ready to play out its deadly mischief.

When they heard the wind ringing toward them, the Teutite drivers turned up their fleece-lined collars, tightened the knots in their scarfs, and fortified themselves with long, burning swigs from their wine jars. The reins went slack as the drivers twisted in their seats to tie down the hide flaps that led inside the wagons, where women and children fought to hold a weak grip on sleep amid the lurching, bobbing cargo lining the wooden floors. Left unattended in their yokes, the oxen trudged on, for they knew the road. And they closed their eyes, for they also knew the wind.

Gushing down between the canyon's steep walls, the wind struck them, oxen and men, square in the face, freezing tears into crystals on their lashes. From the head to the tail of the caravan, the wind tore at the covers of the wagons till the stretched skins vibrated as loudly as drums. It buffeted the carts, lifting wheels off the ground and letting them smash back down, then the wind disappeared into the darkness. There it swirled, gathering its forces like so many floating veils, and circled back.

The wind danced, surged, screamed. It was like an invisible swarm of bees piercing through every crevice of leather and wool, till it found the most vulnerable recesses of human flesh and stung them there, mercilessly. The Teutite drivers squirmed, slapped, cursed, and whipped the oxen in frustration, knowing no one could outrun the wind. Then, suddenly, the gale broke off. The caravan was shuttered in a heavy silence.

Above their heads, the wind flew straight up the sides of the canyon, gaining height for the final plunge that would send the wagons reeling. Racing faster, it skimmed along the boulders, uprooting bushes and tearing out small trees as it climbed higher, ever higher, till it reached the crest and crashed into the great scarred face of Micar, master of the Horlas.

Dazed, the wind tumbled around without direction. It swept up and down the ranks of mutated Horlas that lined the canyon rim, sniffed at their ponies, and twirled around their long, crooked lances. Then, as if it had decided to be mad at being surprised, the wind tore through the horde of warriors.

The wind threw sand in Micar's face, and though his black mare staggered, Micar never blinked. The coarse grains dug deep into the soft, white flesh of his eyes that were already tangled with red roots. But Micar never blinked. He was not afraid of sand. He was not afraid of wind.

Roaring through the Horlas, the wind grabbed at their shields. Rattling their curved swords, it pulled at their tar-coated pigtails. The Horlas took no notice. All eyes were focused on the wagons, all ears tuned to the creak of wooden axles. To them, the cold gust was just a pestering child tugging at their legs. So the wind, deflated by this sudden defeat, dispersed into the night.

Micar watched the caravan in the same way that a mongoose watches the cobra, letting it crawl between the mountains where it cannot coil. There were jugs of aral-root wine sloshing inside those wagons. There were bolts of dyed silk, crates of fragrant incense, tasty spices. And there was diamond-studded gold, rubies with fire frozen inside them. There were women. There were also swords and battle-axes pressed into the leathery hands of the Teutites. But Micar was not afraid of dying. No Horla was.

When a star shot across the black sky to embrace the moon, Luna veiled her blush with a cloud, and the caravan was hidden in the shadows. Micar turned to his left.

There he found Allukah, his fourth wife, astride the Arabian charger he had given her on their wedding day, when she was still young and beautiful and slim. Now, foam had started to leak through the gaps in her brown teeth as her huge arms wrestled with the reins, fighting to keep the charger at the head of the line so she could be first to draw blood. Allukah had filled out into a fierce warrior, swinging a mace so large it took two normal men to lift it, and she struck with accurate blows that could shatter a steel helmet, let alone a fragile skull. She was as strong and terrible as Micar himself, the most terrible of the Horlas. Still, she lacked his self-control, his subtle wisdom, and that was probably the only thing that prevented her from challenging his position as master of the Horlas. And she was the only one strong enough to challenge him. No man could resist Allukah. No man but Micar.

Micar turned to his right, meeting the flint-hard stare of Amurti, the son Allukah had borne him during the four-day pursuit of the Carabor tribe. That was during the War of Clocks. Allukah had left the saddle only long enough to squat, while a thrashing Amurti struggled out into the light. Then, leaving him in the protection of some blue Boroka nomads, she caught up with the Horlas again.

Amurti shared his mother's ruddy, pockmarked skin, and his beaten-copper helmet poured out the same straggly, reddish-black mane of hair. Yet, when Allukah first came to Micar's great hut those many long years ago, she was light skinned and fair. Micar hadn't touched her since she changed. He consoled himself with his other twenty-six wives, and that suited Allukah. She came out only at night to pillage and roam. The daylight hours were spent in her special caves—with her special collection of pets.

At every impatient twitch of Amurti's body, the necklace around his neck clicked and rattled against his flashing breastplate. It was a long, looping string of molars, one for each man Amurti had freed from this earthly struggle. To prove his courage, he extracted these enamel jewels from the squealing jaws of his victim before cutting off the head with a single slice of his axe. Unlike the other Horlas, who shunned armor as clumsy and the sanctuary of cowards, Amurti wore a breastplate of tooled copper. Inscribed on the soft metal were important scenes from his short life: his birth, his first kill, his first marriage. One very large panel was left empty: his future. Amurti insisted he wore the breastplate solely for decoration. In truth, the thin, soft metal offered almost no protection from even a sharp stick. Rather, he wanted to show them all—the Teutites, the

8

Horlas, everybody—that Horlas weren't just a savage pack of stinking barbarians. He wanted to show them that the Horlas deserved respect, that they were capable of building as well as destroying. Amurti's mother had filled his head with these useless, romantic notions, and Micar realized that Amurti fully intended to one day rule the Horlas. That was the reason for the empty panel on the breastplate. And that was also the reason why Micar nursed a feeble hope for Amurti to fall glorious and dead in battle. It would spare Micar the everlasting shame of having to kill his own son.

To either side of Amurti were the twins, Cular and Mishla, who were born identical and remained that way until a well-aimed lance plucked Mishla's eye from its socket. Inconsolable, he had refused to eat or fight until Cular struck out his own eye and made them twins again. Despite their wounds, the image of Micar was branded into their face.

The two brothers were archers, and they insisted that a single eye enhanced their aim by heightening their concentration on every shot. Each carried a bow carved out of the supple leg bones of the mad magician Praxus who had kidnapped them while they were infants and kept them in bondage until they grew big enough to turn on him. Both twins wore helmets that once were skulls of Watutes, the unfortunate race of giants they had helped drive to extinction.

Micar raised a scarred eyebrow when he saw the wolfish face of Maskim, the cretin, slinking around behind his sons. Maskim, immediately noting the master's displeasure, whispered a hasty appeal into the silver-sheathed ears of his mule, begging the beast to be still and stop shaking the sleighbells strung along the animal's shaggy flanks. Without the wind to cover the sound, the chiming would carry as far as the wary

9

Teutite ears, and Micar had no intention of forfeiting the advantage of surprise.

Maskim had also fitted his mule with leather shoes, and atop the animal's head tottered a straw hat woven with freshly cut petunias. Maskim had covered his own head with a wreath of wild ivy and stuffed leaves through the coarse weave of his jerkin to disguise himself as a brother to the tree—a tree riding a mule sheathed in silver and strung with bells. Aluminum earrings and a plastic eyepatch broke through the wisps of mousy hair covering his face to complete Maskim's battle dress. Today, the patch was over his right eye. On the last raid it had covered his left. There was nothing wrong with either eye, but he insisted the patch aided his concentration—just as it did for the twins. Despite this clownish appearance, it would be a mistake to discount this Horla. Maskim was as deadly as gangrene. He had survived many raids, and anyone, on either side, who survived a Horla raid had to be deadly. Maskim hadn't the brains for caution. There wasn't an ounce of sense in his entire warped body.

Maskim's ugliness was eclipsed by a tall rider slicing the thick night air with a scimitar at least five feet long. Micar smiled warmly at the sight of the bearded Careem, who was the distillation of Horla spirit and determination, for, though the warrior had but one arm, he kept his pony in place by pulling the end of his right shoulder. The arm had been severed in battle, while the hand still clutched a sword, by a Somelon, a member of that vicious race of women warriors. The green-eyed Sheryl, whose private vengeance against the Horlas knew no earthly bounds, had left him lying there with his blood spurting life from his arteries. Sure that he was dead, she went on to flush out and exterminate more Horlas. It was hatred for her that had kept his heart pumping, the chance for revenge that kept him alive. Now, his life was dedicated to meeting that gold-haired Somelon again. Only her blood could stop the painful throbbing that clogged his quivering stump.

Filling the remainder of the canyon rim like a row of wild gargoyles on the wall of some medieval castle were the rest of Micar's savage mongrels. Each sat on a pony, since only Micar's family was allowed by tribal law the luxury of a horse. The ponies were quick little mounts that could outstep and outmaneuver any horse, though of course they hadn't the horse's strength and endurance. Standing between the bulky thighs of the Horlas, tan cowlicks hanging to their foreheads, they looked curiously harmless and invited a hand to reach out and brush the hair out of their eyes. Any hand that tried it came back bloody and lighter by a finger or two.

Now the Horlas, their ponies dripping scalps and skulls, turned to Micar. They held their painted leather shields low, confident that even this weak protection would be unnecessary. Their hands clutched for fresh grips around the traditional tools of the Horla trade: battle-axes, spears, studded maces, and jagged chrome javelins. Inbred and mutilated by continuous warfare, their greasy bodies were clothed only in the untanned skins of animals they had slain; those brittle hide robes scraped against the skin until it bled and the wounds festered, then they scraped the scabs. But the Horlas scarcely noticed such petty discomforts, which were just another part of their lives, just like the dawn, dysentery, mange, or lice. They wouldn't lift a mangled, pony-bitten finger to change any of it. No, the Horlas survived, and they didn't do it by compromising, by adapting, or by solving problems. No, they rode right over anything that stood in their way—before it rode over them. They survived by sheer force, taking what they needed, as

11

well as a lot they didn't need, from those too weak to stop them. It was a simple law of evolution, one that had worked so well with animals. In the narrow confines of the Horla's mind, the only difference between rider and pony was that one was on top, the other on the bottom. It wasn't much different from the relationship of Horla women to Horla men—except where Allukah was concerned. The Horlas were a herd of collective impulses that listened to only one voice at a time.

As the moon finally shed its cloudy veil, as the caravan appeared below, that voice roared.

"Spare none!" Micar cried, his sword striking out in the direction of the wagons.

The Horlas plunged down the canyon walls in an avalanche of instinct.

Chapter 2

Scavengers

Buzzing. It started somewhere deep inside the skull, a snake about to hatch, wriggling, gnawing, thrashing against the shell till it cracked. Then the buzzing spread, seeping through the darkness, shredding into the brain, a violent yellow acid leaking into her eyes. She blinked once. Again. Only then did she realize she was staring at the sun.

Slapping at the flies boring into every moist pocket of her body, Sheryl wrenched herself around. The vertebrae in her neck grated like a millstone cracking grain. The pain twisted through her nerves, arching her spine. She shuddered, then drove her face into the sand. Breathing in great lungfuls of the dust she had raised, Sheryl lay there squirming for a long time waiting for her sight to return. Each slow second of that time was measured by the pounding in her head. Yet, not once did she wince, for Somelon warriors never show pain, not even when they are alone.

Gradually, sight trickled back. Summoning the energy, Sheryl propped herself up on her elbows and forced her head to turn one way then the next, as her blonde hair wiped across her soft, white shoulders, smearing the sweat and sand that clung to them. On all sides boulders blocked her crippled view, but she was in no hurry to see more. Sheryl remembered where she was and how she got there, and what was waiting beyond this circle of rocks. It would still be there in an hour, in

13

a day. It would be out there forever, were it not for the jackals, both the two-legged and four-legged kinds, were it not for the buzzards, the flies, and for the modesty with which the earth bandages its wounds with the sifting sands. Sheryl knew there was death strewn on the other side of those rocks, and she held back partly because she had done nothing to prevent it.

Sheryl had been asleep when the raiders struck, curled up like a child, a camp follower along with Kio in the back of the wagon, hiding from the wind. She had let herself drift into his arms. And she enjoyed it. There was no denying that. She had enjoyed it too much. Sheryl had let her guard down, as no Somelon warrior could afford to do. Still, her reflexes had remained alert. As soon as the first war cry pierced the wagon's cover, she was scrambling in the darkness for her sword. The weapon never should have left its sheath—that lapse was unforgivable. But she was ready then, the blade light and eager in her left hand, the winged helmet in her right. While she hesitated there, halfway through the rear flap of the bucking wagon, before she could even slip on the helmet, a club crashed into her temple, sending her flying to the side of the road. Tumbling unconscious into the rocks, she had gone unnoticed in the confusion of slaughter and looting. It was all she could remember until now, except for the buzzing, the molten pain leaking from her head into her neck.

With her sword as a crutch, Sheryl struggled up to sit gratefully on one of the cold rocks. She didn't try to slow the dreams dashing through her brain, because they gave her an excuse not to look any further. But there was really no place to hide. Already, the stench of human flesh, fermenting in the heat of that treacherous sun, was slinking through the air toward her nose. She could put it off no longer.

14

Her arms moved first, unfolding from the protective cradle they held around her steel-incased breasts. Reaching skyward, her limbs carried the aching body along with them until Sheryl stood her full seven feet above the rocky ground. She continued to stretch, the muscles wriggling beneath her skin as she squeezed out the pain. It was an old Somelon trick, passed on by her mother. You twisted the nerves, the muscles, the bones, as you would a wet rag, tighter and tighter, until there was no room left for the pain to hide in. That was one of the few things Sheryl remembered about her mother— along with a dripping mane of golden hair, a distaste for venison, and a brown scar shaped into a six-pointed star beneath her left breast. "Where Cupid's arrow entered," her mother had blushed, "when I met your father." Sheryl knew the arrow had really come from a Horla's bow. Her mother had been a warrior, as every Somelon must be. Then, one night, the Horlas returned, and Sheryl had only her father left to comfort. She still could hear his sobs. They were woven into her eardrums.

As soon as her head cleared, Sheryl took a step. Gratified by a wobbly success, she tried another till she was walking, climbing over the rocks. She kept her green eyes under strict control as she stepped down to the road and waded into the debris, not letting them stray to the right or left. Water was the primary concern. She needed it soon if she was to survive, so she couldn't let anything sidetrack her till the thirst was quenched.

She located a water bag on the side of an overturned wagon; it was like a dried prune dangling in the stagnant air. The bag had been slit open, and a small, sun-frozen puddle in the cracked dirt below attested to the cool liquid that had once filled the bladder. Sheryl slipped a hand in through the slit, and her fingers carefully explored the interior. A few drops still clung to the bottom, so she spread the bag apart and forced her head inside. Her parched tongue and lips slid over the smooth skin, licking, chasing each precious drop, and sucking it into her mouth. When she pulled her head out into the light again, her lips were glistening, but the sun soon dried them. The skin cracked. Sheryl ran her tongue over salty lips and released her eyes to roam.

The lead wagon had gotten as far as the end of the canyon. There, at the tail, Sheryl found the same scene. The raiders had waited until the caravan filled the road between the canyon walls, then they sealed it inside at both ends by slaying the animals that drew the wagons. The yokes of the middle wagons were empty. Those oxen were probably the only survivors of the raid besides Sheryl. But it was only a stay of execution. Once the raiders reached camp, there would be a feast to celebrate the victory. The main course would be oxtail soup.

Now that her eyes had the freedom of their sockets, they discovered a Teutite merchant sprawled at her feet, his eyes open wide as though staring up under the short skirt of her tunic, the only thing Sheryl wore beneath her armor. His eyes were dark and already filling with cream-colored eggs of the bluebottle flies. Soon enough, maggots would poke their squirming heads out through the sockets and slide back into the moist flesh when they found the dry air waiting to grab them.

Next to the merchant lay what was left of a gypsy driver. His gold-swirled shirt was shredded and dirty, and where his vest had slid aside there were rows of bright red punctures. The driver's head was twisted, his tongue pushed out. A raider had grabbed hold of the scarf around his neck, pulled him from the seat, and dragged him behind his pony, while the other raiders

16

pierced him through with their lances. Where his right ear once held a rhinestone earring, there was only a shredded, brown hole.

Sheryl kicked over the swollen body of the merchant. His ear had been cut off as well. Sheryl knew the meaning of this mutilation.

"Horlas," she hissed.

Micar had led them here. Sheryl's lips curled, showing just the tips of her teeth. She looked toward the desert, the direction from which the Horlas always came, the direction they fled after wasting and butchering what civilized men had built, what Somelons had protected. She spat and cursed herself. If she hadn't been so weak, if she hadn't let Kio pull her guard down, she would have killed many Horlas last night, maybe even Micar himself, or that slimy cow of a wife, Allukah. Sheryl imagined the thrill she would feel to split open that fat belly of hers like a rotten watermelon.

Once Sheryl's head cleared completely, signs of the Horlas surfaced everywhere. Scalped corpses bristled with the short, featherless shafts that were the arrows of Cular and Mishla. Shattered, bloody jaws had surrendered their teeth for a place in Amurti's necklace. Sheryl shivered, filled with a rage that came too late. She never should have listened to him. She never should have relaxed. If it wasn't for Kio . . .

Kio!

Sheryl's mouth softened as she looked around for the wagon they had hired. There it was, a tall, blue and gold wagon, the only one with springs between the wheels and body. It was a sinful luxury. Kio had picked it because he wanted her to be comfortable. Comfortable. A Somelon warrior. The very idea was ludicrous. Sheryl stepped through the corpses, swatting away the buzzing flies as she went.

Behind the wagon, she found her helmet already half covered by the sand. One of the eagle's wings on its side had been trampled by a pony's hoof, though the smooth silver surface of the dome was unscratched. Pulling the helmet out of the sand, she pressed it to the back of her neck. The hot metal took some of the tension out of the muscles there.

When her hand touched the flap on the rear of the wagon, Sheryl paused a moment to prepare herself. The last few weeks had worn down her resistance and hopelessly tangled the direction of her life that once was so straight and clear. She was thankful now that she had listened to one of Kio's suggestions and sent her father's body on ahead. Kio had been stronger than her then, had shown her how to rest while he took care of the details of embalming, shipping, and satisfying all the petty laws civilized men placed on everything, even the dead. Kio said it would be too much of a strain on her (as though too much meant anything to a Somelon) to go through the breast-beating ordeal of leading a funeral cortege through the heat of the summer desert. In fact, Sheryl never had any intention of doing such a thing. It was not the Somelon way. Yet, she let Kio run around while she enjoyed the small luxuries of being just a woman for the first time in her life. And thanks to Kio, her father's body would be safe in the rolling meadows of Varman by now. Had it fallen into the clutches of the Horlas, they would have desecrated the corpse, just to prove they were not afraid of death.

A tug on the flap released a wave of heated air that carried a swarm of flesh-eating horseflies along with it. After the putrid odor, the first thing Sheryl let herself notice was her trunk thrown into a corner, its lid smashed in. It was empty. Her father's tools were gone, and so was the exquisite armor of her mother. The discovery wasn't much of a surprise. Horlas wouldn't leave that kind of treasure behind. There had been a breastplate beaten out of cold steel to hug the contours of her mother's body with the skill and precision of hands that intimately understood both the metal and the body—her father's hands. Covered with a layer of silver and trimmed with gold, a ruby eye tipped each breast, an emerald nose the navel, and at the hips a silver mouth curled into a smile. A beard of leather strips fringed the bottom. There had been a hawk's-head helmet to match, gauntlets, shinplates, all fashioned with the same, meticulous craft, the same intricate love. A metalsmith his whole life, Sheryl's father's skill was famous far beyond the borders of Philistria. Princes and emirs came from the five corners of the world, from as far east as Abyssinia and as far north as the frozen steppes where the sun never sets, all to have him set their jewels, build impenetrable armor, or to cast the golden death masks of lovers and friends. One day, a Somelon warrior had come down from Mt. Palus and asked him to fashion a new set of armor. It was to celebrate her taking command of the fortress. But she was never to wear it in battle, for, though she was close to seven feet tall and he closer to five, they both fell immediately and irretrievably in love. Yes, it was a storybook romance, and the sweet memory of it had a lot to do with why Sheryl's father had liked Kio so much when they met.

Kio.

Sheryl scanned the interior of the wagon with her eyes, seeking the scent of Kio's body on the hot air with her nose. Against the far wall, a body lay sprawled and bloody. Sheryl crawled inside the wagon.

It wasn't Kio. Instead, Sheryl found a young Teutite woman. Horlas can usually be relied upon to spare young females and drive them over the desert with the oxen, to satisfy a different kind of hunger, perhaps, bot to share the same fatal reward. This particular woman, it seemed, had been pregnant, too weak to make the long trek across the dunes, too swollen to give good pleasure. So she lay there now with a huge hole in her middle where they had cut the baby out. Her treasure was gone. She was as empty as Sheryl's trunk.

The body of the baby was nowhere in sight. It might have been taken as a pathetic trophy or simply thrown out for the hyenas. Or the tales of Horla cannibalism might have some truth in them.

Kio wasn't anywhere inside the wagon either, and outside the air seemed to be clogged with a heavy pollen, a pollen so heavy it worked its way into Sheryl's eyes, irritating her membranes and releasing tears that washed the pollen grains away in small rivulets down her cheeks. She almost looked as if she were crying, though Somelon warriors, of course, never cry. There was no one there to see except Shamask, the sun, the enemy of all Somelons, so he could only be expected to lie about what he saw.

Kio.

Why hadn't the fool listened to her? Sure, he was a successful sculptor who had carved a comfortable life for himself inside the great walled city of Centropolis. It was quite an accomplishment in the world of men, where there were laws and rules and a myth named justice, a dream called security. Everyone knew that was not the real world. It definitely wasn't the unvarnished world Sheryl knew, the world they had built those walls to seal out. Kio had lived in a place where he could survive for seventy years or more without once taking the kinds of risks Sheryl took every day. He should have stayed behind those walls. Hadn't she told him to? Hadn't she warned him? But no, that made too much sense. What good was sense when it had to stand up to a man's inflated ego? She didn't understand him, he said. She was only a woman. Then the blood rushed to her cheeks as quickly as if he had struck her with his fists. She hated him, and perhaps it was that second of hate that had sealed them together forever.

Sheryl knew there was no way she could avoid taking the full blame for what had happened. A Somelon had no excuse for falling under the spell of a man. To Somelons, men were a necessary evil, required to produce more Somelons and, occasionally, a little amusement. They might give an hour's diversion, a couple of twinges of excitement at best, but they were like a song, a dance. Once you sang the song, once you danced the dance, you went on to the next, found a new step, a livelier tune. Singing and dancing were games, unworthy of concentration. So were men. A Somelon's concentration was reserved for one purpose and one purpose only: war. Sheryl's mother had loved her father, and it had destroyed them both. Sheryl couldn't expect to repeat that mistake and go unpunished.

Yet, how could she help herself? How could any woman resist Kio? Even if Somelons weren't just any women, behind those fortified walls of Centropolis, it was too easy to shut out the lightning bolts of death, the storm of survival raging on the other side. Kio's studio shut out the wind, muffled the thunder until it was just a distant rumble that was easily overwhelmed by the sigh of his chisel slicing a smooth line over the marble. Kio's knives scratched intricate scrawls and details into the stone as if it were soap. Under repeated blows of his hammer, small dusty chips flaked away. She had watched the entire transformation of a shapeless rock into a plump cherub, yet somehow she was shocked when her hand reached out and found the stone cold, hard. Maybe she expected it to yield ever so slightly under the pressure of her fingertips, as if it were flesh as white as her own. And maybe that's the reason she slid her hand over the statue till it touched his arm, warm, soft, and dusted with powdered rock. Oh, his hands were strong, all right. Used to working stone, they had no trouble working over the firm contours of a Somelon's body. They probed, molded her milk-white flesh into a passion she should never have experienced, for it made her forget that world outside, made her think she could ignore it. She had only been fooling herself. That was brutally clear as soon as they left those protective walls behind. Kio was a gentle fawn in a hostile world of predators. Instead of protecting him, instead of forcing him to stay behind, she had curled up next to him in the back of a Teutite wagon, like a mongrel puppy. It was her fault. All of it. They would all be alive if Sheryl had been on guard.

Rounding the corner of a supply wagon, Sheryl surprised a pack of jackals feasting on a corpse. It was a natural, a common enough sight, these beasts feeding on the extravagance, the greed of men, and it was a sight that normally wouldn't have earned an extra blink of her eye. Yet, it might be Kio's flesh dripping from their bone-crushing jaws. The thought drove her mad. With a single stride, she landed in the center of the pack. Shrieking, she grabbed the neck of a quivering bitch and tore out handfuls of her mangy, striped fur. The wild beasts snapped, their anal sacs secreting the stench of fear. Sheryl growled back, snatching their flea-infested bodies off the ground and flinging them far into the jagged rocks to crash down in a rain of piercing yelps. Sheryl was burning with rage, but as soon as she recognized the feeling, she forced herself to stop.

It took the full measure of her control to instantly

freeze the muscles of her body, even as the jackals circled around, nipping at her bare legs, though they didn't yet dare to bite. She had to clear her mind, strip it of these sudden compulsions. Now, more than ever, she had to keep her discipline. When the anger evaporated, so did the jackals, for they recognized the new power that had condensed in her.

With calm patience, Sheryl moved from corpse to rotting corpse, examining each one to see who it was and how it had died. The jackals' prey was beyond identification, though it was obviously not Kio. In one of the supply wagons, she uncovered a stowaway, with his throat slashed clear to the spine. That was a harsh penalty for the ride the boy had stolen, an exorbitant price. Then again, death is never a bargain.

Sheryl picked over grandmothers with their grey heads clubbed in. There were men and women disemboweled and strangled with their own intestines. Every one of them was missing a right ear. When the search finally wound down to its stomach-surging conclusion, she hadn't located Kio's body. The jackals might have dragged it away, though that wasn't very likely, what with all the other bodies to choose from. So, it appeared that Kio, for whatever reason, had been taken captive. It was not a conclusion that gave Sheryl any real hope for finding him alive. In fact, it was probably the worst of several bad alternatives.

Sheryl walked to the rim of the great Sugar Desert that lay beyond the clogged mouth of the canyon. By this time, the Horlas were on their own side of the scorched plane, secure in their squalid village and fighting over the spoils. Soon, they would be drunk on root wine. Then they would begin to murder one another. It would be a simple matter to take them by surprise, to recover her mother's armor and Kio—if he were still in one piece. A simple matter, were it not for the Sugar Desert standing between them. That was her opponent now, forty miles of dessicated powder with scarcely a weed, barely a boulder strong enough to stand up to the blasting erosion of the wind. Crossing during the heat of the day was impossible. She would have to wait until Shamask, the sun, worked his way under the horizon before she could place a foot on the sand. Her vengeance would have to wait, too. Until then, she would spend the time preparing for the battle that was always waiting for a Somelon warrior.

Sheryl hadn't eaten since leaving Centropolis yesterday morning. Already, her muscles were demanding their daily ration of meat, the red meat of a strong animal. She turned back to the caravan.

The two oxen the Horlas had slain would be more than enough for her. When the flies sensed her coming, they surrendered all claims on the carcasses. The unique vibrations of a Somelon preparing for battle were prohibitive to them. It was an awareness aggregated in their genes, and they were much too wise to ignore it.

Standing over one of the carcasses, Sheryl drew the sword from its sheath and sighted down its length. Already, small, brown flecks of rust were spreading over the blade. They had both been idle too long, dwelling in the sluggish company of men, wallowing in distractions. That was not the way a Somelon should live. Both her father's death and Kio had extracted a toll of her strength. Now she needed to regain that strength, to give it direction. When Sheryl's hands wrapped around the thick handle of the sword, the amalgam of muscle and steel re-created the old alchemy. The power of a warrior pulsed back into her palms, surged up her arms, and raised the sword over her head. With one stroke, she sliced the carcass in half and carried it to the shade of an overturned wagon.

Sheryl could have taken fire from her bag and roasted the meat. That would have been the civilized thing to do. There was plenty of wood in the wagons. With the Horlas on the other side of the desert, there was no need to hide the smoke. Any other visitors would be welcomed to share her meat, to fight over it, or to die. Nor did she fear the eyes of strangers after she stripped off her armor and left her untanned skin exposed. Rather, she needed the water that formed the bulk of the flesh. So, sitting on a crate, she braided her blonde hair into a rope and ate the meat raw, cold, without really tasting it. The process was purely mechanical. Raising the meat to her mouth, she bit, tore, chewed, then swallowed. She ate not for pleasure, but to supply food for her muscles, liquid for her organs.

When the gristly meal was done, her stomach swollen, Sheryl left the shade to expose the full length of her body to the sun. It was almost a challenge to Shamask's power. The ivory surface of her body was immune to his searing rays. It scattered them so efficiently that the radiant heat could do no more than try to evaporate the beads of sweat squirming out of her pores before they slid down her face. As they ran over her neck, the drops collected together, spreading into a sheet over her breasts, then dripped off the tips of her nipples. Just grazing her navel, the drops became tangled in the small patch of blonde hair below until they dribbled down her thighs. The sunrays chased the rivulets around her body, and the swirl of air raised by the pursuit cooled and soothed her.

Sheryl took her sword in hand and held it erect. With the plaited bundle of her hair, she wiped the maroon ox blood from its surface. The gentle friction of those golden fibers rubbed away every congealed trace of the blood, though once they had run the full length of the blade, a trail of rust still traced over the steel. In the rubble between her toes she found a whetstone, black and smooth. She held it against the blade and slid it over the surface, pressing the stone lightly at first, pausing to give special attention to a particularly eroded spot, then passing on to another. Up one side she went, then down the other, polishing, working her way out toward the edge. When she reached that part of the blade that tapered into a cutting wedge, she slid the stone faster, in long, even strokes, while she lubricated it with her spit. Her hand vibrated, honing, smoothing over the blade's full length until the steel gleamed, a razor's edge.

Touching the tip of the blade to her tongue, Sheryl smiled when she felt it pierce easily through the skin. After she wrapped the handle with fresh strips of leather, the weapon was ready.

Sheryl now had to purify her body. There was no water for bathing, but the clean, hot desert sand was as good as any perfumed balm. She lay face down in the dunes, wriggling to push her breasts and hips deep into the cleansing grains. While she worked her body through the sand, she slowly twisted until her face pointed skyward again. The blood, the oil, and the grime were scrubbed from her skin as her muscles were massaged by the penetrating heat. Sheryl ran the sand through her hair, over her face, scouring, absorbing till every pore and fiber was immaculate. Then she rested there until Shamask shrunk from the bare challenge of her beauty and he hid behind the horizon. Only then did Sheryl rise out of the sand.

As the cold wind drifted in off the desert again, it found Sheryl in full armor, and it could have cursed itself for not coming a few minutes sooner. It lingered to watch her straighten the bent wing on her helmet and slip it over her golden hair. The sword was slammed into its sheath.

Picking up a bundle of meat, Sheryl strode into the Sugar Desert. The wind followed on the heels of her fur boots.

Chapter 3

In the Sugar Desert

It was almost like slipping into a moonlit pool. Sheryl made little more than a ripple as she waded into the rapidly chilling air of the Sugar Desert. Gentle currents lifted her hair off her armored shoulders, then circled round to her nose to release the enchanted fragrances of flowers and herbs. As it shimmered over the silver horizon, the breeze had transported the scents all the way across the unbroken plain of the desert, and now it doled them out in carefully calculated measures, offering just a whiff before snatching them back. When the sweet smells dispersed, others rushed in to fill their places: the oil musks of creatures sliding into the night like crocodiles from the river bank.

In the beginning, the only sound was the steady, muffled splash of Sheryl's furred boots over the sand, the only light the greenish glow of the Najucular stones. Sheryl flowed through the darkness, and it welcomed her inside its folds. The head had already vaporized out of the ground, drawing with it the life of newts and dragons whose scaly bodies sank to the bottom to await the rush of dawn. But there were other creatures ready to scurry over their cold-blooded bodies, and only at night, when they thought they could escape the blood-boiling death of the sun, did they stir. Wet noses poked gingerly out of deep, damp burrows. Small dark eyes soaked in the moonlight, then squeezed it back out again as they wrung the atmosphere for traces of food.

Scattering eager cries, they scrambled until the entire floor of the desert was sown with stars from one skyline to the next. The night above merged into the night below to surround Sheryl in a vast globe of sparkling black velvet.

Her ears cocked and strained through the sound of her own quick breaths, the Somelon searched for warnings, vibrating signals as she stalked through the scorched landscape. In an hour she covered nine miles, which left thirty to go before there would be any shelter from the implacable Shamask, the sun racing around the earth to catch her. It was then that something shot out, wrapped itself around her ankle, and pulled her legs out from under her.

Before Sheryl's face even bit into the sand, the sword was out of its sheath and raised above her head, poised to fall. She spun around, her legs still in the grip of a creature she could not see. The thing was down there, somewhere beyond her foot. That was where the sword would strike.

"Sheryl," a weak voice whistled. "You put that sword down. Put it down, I say. Right now!"

A pair of glowing red eyes floated above her knee, then glided closer. Her sword could have cut right through them, yet she hesitated to slay something before knowing that it was, especially when they something knew her name.

"Sheryl," the thing whistled again. She let the sword ease down to the ground. Sheryl knew many of the creatures hunting the desert, and one of them was Kryl.

"Your old eyes charm the darkness better than mine," she said, shoking back a laugh. It wasn't because she was glad to see him, because she really couldn't see him. She recognized the rasping voice that had barked so often in her childhood. "And those eyes of yours almost got you dead."

"Ach, you wouldn't hurt Kryl."

"Not if I was presented with the choice, old man. But you could have been split into bookends before I found out who you were."

"What's happened to those celebrated Somelon senses? Do the troubadours lie? Why, my stiff ears knew it was you as soon as they heard those big feet clomping on the roof of my underground lair."

"How would you like one of those big feet in your big mouth?" The laugh came full now. She took fire out of her bag in order to see his face. Somehow, she didn't remember it having quite so many wrinkles. Both his eyebrows and hair were frosted with a fine coating of dust. "Get something to burn. We'll make a fire. I have some meat."

"Are you sure? A fire will be seen for miles."

"Of course I'm sure, old man. No one's on my trail. I'm doing the chasing. The hare doesn't even know the hound has the scent."

"Not yet he don't."

The years had made them shy of each other, so they sat on opposite sides of the kindling and peat, issuing instructions, demonstrating, fanning, as though neither had ever lit a fire before. Once the meat began to roast, dripping flares of fat, their flinches were a bit too exaggerated to be comfortable.

Sheryl took only a small chunk of the beef. She munched it slowly, with delicate bites, letting Kryl get way ahead of her, for he looked to be a stranger to food. Anyway, she wanted to look over while he was busy eating. The fire's glow spread reverently over Kryl's ancient face as though it feared the brittle skin might crack even under the softest glance of light. Tentatively, it touched his chin, then his forehead, though it dared not enter the hollows of his cheeks, the deep furrows of his brow. Even light wasn't bold enough to penetrate the secrets clawed into his face by so many years.

"You look terrible," she scolded. "When I last saw you—"

"When you last saw me!" He blew the words out of his nose, wiping his mouth with a bony, dusty arm. "When you last saw me, your baby fat had melted away to leave you a broom handle topped with cracked straw. Now you are a Somelon warrior, and the stories of your exploits arrive a week before you do, reaching even my godforsaken hovel. When you last saw me, my hair was pitch black and shorn as close as an autumn lamb. My too-often-fed body was draped with silk robes embroidered with silver dragons and girdled with the golden cords of the magi." Kryl pulled the shreds of his clothes together. "Much has changed since you last saw me."

"My father is dead." Her eyes jerked toward the darkness, denying any responsibility for the words. In the distance, the lights of another caravan bobbed like a fleet of ships crossing a low sea.

"I know." The old man's voice was even. He dropped the rest of the meat into the flames and chewed for a long time before being able to swallow what was already in his mouth.

"You should have eaten all of it. It would give you back your strength."

"Strength? Why do I need strength? I'm no warrior. I'm not chasing anyone, except maybe your father, and maybe I'll catch up with him soon."

"You knew about his death, yet you didn't come."

"Come where?" His eyes shot up and pinned her. "I knew your father while he was a man. What did that

31

have to do with some rotting hunk of flesh he discarded? We shared many goblets of aral wine in our time, so many that I still have the headaches when I wake up in the morning. Why should I come now? I was there when you were born, when your father's hands shook so bad he couldn't even close his fingers. It was I who pulled you out of your mother's womb. It was I who tied the cord and cut it with my own teeth while your little feet kicked me in the face because you were so modest, embarrassed at letting me see you naked." There was a gleam floating in his eye. He might have expected her to blush. She did not.

"I was there when your sister died. I was there the night the Horlas came, when your mother—"

Kryl's mouth raced so quickly through the past that, when his ears eventually caught up, he broke off abruptly. Minutes passed. When finally he spoke again, his voice could barely be heard above the crackling fire.

"I gave you and your father all I could when you needed it. Now he is dead, and you don't need anyone's help. You've grown strong, stronger than any of us."

"Then it's my turn to help you." Sheryl moved around the fire to sit closer to him.

"It's too late for that. If you'd been here two years ago, you might have chased the Horlas away. As it was, they stripped off my robes and took my horse. Then, just for fun, they shattered the bones in my legs. They took turns with the club. They enjoyed hearing me scream. I'm a good screamer. They enjoyed watching me crawl. And they wouldn't kill me, even when I begged them to. I guess I'm not a good beggar. Anyway, it would have spoiled their sport."

Kryl pulled back the tattered skirt of his lizard-skin robe to show the two gnarled stumps growing out of his hips. Then he lifted the flap of hair on the right side of his head. The ear was gone.

"Yes, I survived, Sheryl. I was too much of a coward to die alone. I burrowed into the ground like a gopher to escape Shamask, our enemy. At night, I slither out to grab whatever runs by. I eat it, no matter what it is. I can't afford to be choosy."

"I'm sorry, Kryl." She put a hand out to touch one of the stumps. He slapped it away.

"A Somelon is never sorry, Sheryl. Didn't your mother teach you that?"

"There is so much she never had a chance to teach me. The rest of the Somelons seem to have disappeared from the face of the earth. Were you there when the Horlas murdered my mother?"

Even in that weak light you could see his mottled skin pucker.

"I was there."

"And what did you do?"

"I did nothing."

Sheryl exchanged a bitter silence with him then. They both held their ground, unable to move together or to part, even when the smoke curled round their bodies to pierce their eyes and noses. Ultimately, it took all of Kryl's strength to reach out and run his hand over Sheryl's bare arm. The small golden hairs bristled in the firelight.

"You're after Micar."

"I'm always after the Horlas."

"This time it's different." Kryl tried to turn her face to his. She was too much for him. "This time they've stolen from you."

"They stole my mother long ago."

"Yes. You were very young then. The old wounds heal, in spite of our picking at them. Sure, they leave scars. But the scars don't show in our eyes. This is a fresh wound."

"My mother's armor that my father—"

"More than that."

"My father's tools."

"More."

"There is this man. . ." She only started to say it.

"Sheryl!" Kryl drooled, rocking back and forth. The way he did it made her feel ashamed, though it wasn't clear why.

"A Somelon chasing after a man? Have you gone mad? A Somelon has no time to waste on men. Look what a man did to your mother. She gave up everything for your father, and what did it prove? Are you aware that she was groomed to take over command at Mount Paulus?"

"But the Somelons deserted that post years ago. They retreated into the hard country, and I've never been able to pick up their trail."

"Why do you think they deserted it? Do you think they wanted to give it up? The Somelons held that fortress since the end of the Great Mushroom War. It was the one stronghold of incorruptible light in this black hole of terror that is the known world. They held out against the Horlas and their allies, every siege, every treachery. Do you think they wanted to give it up? No, they didn't. But Vocar was their general, and even Somelon generals don't live forever. Of course, she selected a successor when she first took command. The baby girl she chose was raised apart from the rest, a queen bee fed royal jelly, given special privileges—and special duties. This special girl turned into a woman more capable than Vocar herself. But then this anointed one spit in their faces. This anointed one debased herself by transferring her loyalty, her talents to a common man. When Vocar heard of it, the shock put her right into her grave. Demoralized and without a replacement for their commander, the Somelons were forced to abandon Mount Palus as indefensible.''

"And that anointed one was my mother. Is that what you're trying to say?''

"Yes, Sheryl. That is why you've become such a great warrior. Every Somelon takes the traits of her mother, no matter what kind of fool her father was. Sometimes, even, Somelons are born without fathers. It happens. Not often, but it happens. The Somelons are the fiercest warriors the world has ever known, and your mother was the ultimate of the breed. Yet she had a single flaw no one recognized until it was too late to correct it. That was a vulgar vulnerability to romance. All those years of promise, the pure ideals of the Somelons, and the hopes of every decent man or woman—they counted for nothing once she laid her green eyes on your father. They all evaporated like so much mist. Your mother sold us all out cheap. No, Sheryl, the Horlas didn't kill your mother. They just happened to be there at the right time. It could have been anything. Truth is, your mother destroyed herself, and she took the rest of us with her. Now, Sheryl, I'm afraid for you. You have the same flaw.''

"Love is not a flaw." As soon as the words left her lips, the mocking song of the jackals began. It came from the direction of the caravan. The jackals were having their revenge.

"It is for you. No man can resist a Somelon, so we cannot blame him. But she has a sacred obligation to preserve herself from his taint. A Somelon uses a man to satisfy her needs, to give a little pleasure in between battles, and, when the time is right, to create more Somelons. She must never allow a man to become one of those needs. All men must be treated the same by her, like beasts of burden, like pets—kindly, of course, but never blurring the line between who is master and who serves."

Sheryl looked hard at the old man. Once he'd been a powerful force in her life, nudging her in the right direction even when her rapidly growing body and personality rebelled. Now she seemed to detect something new in him.

"Why, Kryl. You're jealous of him."

She might have pinched him the way he winced. All the fight went out of him. He slumped low, deflated.

"It's probably true. I have no claim on you. We don't even share the same blood."

She crept up next to him and gathered the withered, gray head into her arms, pressing his face between her steel-sheathed breasts. Kryl kissed one of those pointed cones, and his lips shivered from the cold he tasted. She showed no sign that she noticed.

"All men are children," Sheryl murmured, stroking the place where his ear had been.

"And you do your best to keep us that way."

"Certainly. You'd have it no other way. Even my father. My mother was gone, then you went away, and still he refused to leave our little hut in the Varman Valley. The Horlas came back, again and again, but they couldn't drive him away. Sometimes, I think he half expected my mother to ride in one day and chase them away. Then, everything would be as it was. All those nights we spent huddled together under the floor of the hut, listening to the Horlas smashing and looting the few things we had. I don't know why they bothered to come back. It didn't seem worth the effort."

"The Horlas don't need an excuse to destroy. They enjoy it so."

"I guess you're right. We would crawl out and start rebuilding, then the Horlas would come tearing back to knock it down again. The whole thing made no sense.

To me it was a stupid game without rules, though I was never cruel enough to attack my father's hopes.''

"Your armor is cold," Kryl snuggled close.

"Not nearly as cold as the grave, old man." Sheryl transferred his head to her lap. He rubbed his stubbly face against the smooth skin of her legs, like a cat.

"Even after I grew strong enough to chase the Horlas away, he wouldn't let me face them. I almost went mad when he made me promise not to fight them. Hiding in the cellar while I heard them smashing and laughing, just inches away, I could have screamed! Why, I even accused him of protecting the Horlas. That was a hard vow to keep.''

"Yet, you're after the Horlas now."

"My father is dead. He took the vow with him. Others have replaced it. You see, after one particularly vicious raid, we crawled out to survey the ruins, to end the agony of the animals they tortured. I'd already begun sifting through the smoking debris, looking for anything the Horlas might have missed, when, with a great sigh, he ordered me to stop. We packed his tools, my mother's armor, and we made the trip to Centropolis. It was there I met Kio.''

"Kio? The man?"

"The way you say 'man' makes it sound downright degenerate. You're a traitor to your own sex." She tried to laugh. When it didn't come, she punished him with a sharp tug of his hair. Kryl yelled.

"Ouch!" He rolled out of her lap into the dust, where he laid without moving.

"I am loyal only to my friends, and you happen to be the last one I have left. So I'll tell you again. Let the man go!''

"How can I make you understand? Kio isn't an ordinary man. Even my father called him 'son' the first time they met."

"Son!" He snickered, fingering the stumps that had once been his legs. "A son is a poor man's feeble bid for immortality, a petty vanity, for the world forgets every man sooner or later. Every man wants a son, just as every man hates to die."

"You mean my father was disappointed when I was born?"

"Don't be ridiculous. A daughter is a miniature goddess. But a man can relax with a son, knowing the child has so much to learn, so little time to do it. Then the father is the god, at least till the son grows big enough to challenge him. Women are born wise. Their bodies change, but they keep that innate perception of life men never really grasp. A man has to struggle, learn from his mistakes. It takes many years before he can reason, more before he can survive on his own. It's a contest that leaves him exhausted, and he can't afford to rest. He's always scrambling to fill the gaps, plug the leaks. All the while, there is a woman sitting demurely, waiting, wondering what took him so long to achieve so little. Why do you think we're all awkward and embarrassed when we stand in front of a woman? With a Somelon, the whole thing becomes a tragedy. A man fools himself till he believes he is worthy of an ordinary woman, and she, in her wisdom, lets him believe it. But trying to earn a Somelon is like trying to scale a sheer wall of granite with your bare hands. You only get so far before you slip. Then it's all straight down."

"Kio is a sculptor. He works wonders with granite."

"Don't make light of it, Sheryl. Somelons destroy men."

"Like my mother destroyed my father?"

"They destroyed each other. She made too great a sacrifice for him, one he could never redeem. The

38

burden would have bowed any man's shoulders. It crushed them both."

Sheryl watched him shift sand from one hand to the other. The dust turned the palms red and pasty. It might have been dried blood.

"I don't understand this, Kryl. You say a lot, but you leave more unsaid. If there is something you're hiding from me, I wish you'd bring it out into the open. I deserve to know."

"I can only warn you and hope you will trust me. Your father knew he was going to die, so he looked for somebody to take his place in your life. In desperation, he picked this Kio. Sheryl, you can't base your future on the actions of a sick, desperate man."

"Kio is the desperate one now. Without me he's lost."

"And with you?"

"Your question will be answered *after* I catch the Horlas."

Sheryl stood up. She was so tall that her head was lost in the darkness above the fire.

"Yes, when I saw the Horlas, they had no male captives."

Kryl looked up to where Sheryl's face should be. There was a short pause before she spoke.

"They were here?"

"And there. They came thundering over my burrow a night ago, shaking the earth till my yellow teeth rattled. There was no male captive, I tell you."

"You're sure they were Horlas?"

"I know the Horlas, Sheryl."

"You saw Micar?"

"Yes. I told you."

"And Allukah?"

The muscles in Kryl's face tightened.

"I saw no male captive."

With the speed of a meteorite entering the earth's atmosphere, Sheryl's face dropped out of the sky. She grabbed him and shook him till the old head bobbled on his shoulders.

"Tell me. Did you see Allukah?"

"Yes, damn it. Yes, I saw her."

She relaxed her grip. He collapsed.

"You lie badly, old man."

"Sheryl, you can have any man. Let Allukah have this one. Don't let your pride drive you—"

"Why are you protecting her? You sound like my father now. A Somelon can take the Horlas easily, even Allukah. Why are you trying to stop me?"

"Don't be a fool. I beg you, on your father's name. Leave off this chase. It will cost you more than you can pay."

"I am not afraid of Horlas. I am not afraid of Allukah."

Sheryl muttered as she crawled back to her own side of the fire. Most of the stars had left the brightening sky. The beasts returned to their burrows, leaving only the luminous Najucular stones to break the blanket of darkness still trapped on the ground.

"It's not a question of your courage in battle alone. Suppose you get pregnant?"

Kryl noticed how deeply that word penetrated. It gave him hope.

"You've thought of that already, I see."

"Yes," she bit her lips so hard they began to bleed.

"I don't have to tell you what they could mean. Alone, unprotected, you could die when the time comes. Look, I never asked a favor of you before, did I? In all those years? Well, I'm asking you now. I'm demanding it. You owe me, Sheryl. Let Allukah go!"

Sheryl scanned the horizon. Already, Shamask was stretching his arms over the fringe. She knew Allukah, like most savage beasts, was a nocturnal creature. By now, she'd be scrambling for a safe place to waste out the day. Sheryl would have a good chance of catching up if she started now.

She rose to her feet again.

"It's too late for you to go on, Sheryl. Spend the day in my burrow with me. We'll get to the root of this foolishness."

"It's too late for talk."

"Don't be stubborn. You can't cross the desert while the sun is shining."

"The Jibway Caves!" Sheryl stomped her foot. "That's where they found the son of Tretus before Allukah took him as a pet. That's where I'll be before the sun sets tonight."

"He'll be dead by then. Listen to an old man!"

"Here. This will keep you fit till I come back for you. Stay in your burrow tonight."

She threw a bag into his lap. From the blood that had soaked through the weave, he knew it held more meat.

Sheryl pulled her belt tight, flattening her stomach. She would eat nothing till she found Allukah.

"Sheryl!" the old man cried, beating his fist into the ground. But she had already left the ring of light and was racing across the dunes.

"If you come back at all," the old man sputtered to himself scattering the fire, "you will have lost more than you knew you had."

Then Kryl slithered down into the entrance of his hole and slid the steel cover over his head.

Chapter 4

The Spoils of War

The only light in the cave seeped out of a smoking torch hammered into the wall. At the base of the torch, a milky mix of water trickled out of the limestone to splash on Allukah's matted hair. She was sprawled on the stone floor beneath it, where she could watch him as she drank. With each swallow or belch, the ravenous tumor of her body swelled, then spread back over the cool rock like hot wax as the gas passed out of her. Two enormous breasts hung down as far as the crease in the great globe of her belly, two melons dangling inside loose skin sacks that heaved as her whizzing breath bubbled through the aral-root wine she poured into a mouthful of rotten teeth. The elixir spilled out over her dimpled chin to run along the gutters in her bullish neck. She smeared it into the skin till her chest was a warted swirl of blue grease. All the while, those jaundiced eyes stayed riveted on him, watching, studying as she licked her flap lips and planned the next outrage she would practice on this young, smooth body she had stolen.

There are still some people who insist it's impossible for a woman to rape a man. If Kio had ever been foolish enough to swallow that lie, he had atoned for it by this time. Allukah had shown him her side of the argument. She had forced his muscles and organs to perform in ways that went beyond physical possibilities, beyond the simply repulsive, and so far beyond what was mentally tolerable that he could never go back to being a man again—not the kind of man he had once been. But then he had no reason to believe he would ever get a chance to try, to live another day, another hour. Allukah had the power to end it all with a single slice of her knife, a casual blow from her mace, as she had demonstrated to him when she made him watch the execution of his predecessor in this subterranean menagerie. No, Kio hadn't any reason at all to believe anything anymore, except that the agony hadn't ended yet. He could see that much in Allukah's eyes. She wanted to drain the life right out of him, then discard the empty husk.

Kio wrenched his head away, breaking the link between their eyes. Searching the void above for the soot-covered ceiling, he tried again to block all of this out of his mind. The images of Allukah pursued him no matter which way he turned. Her hairy paws, those pendulous breasts smacking him in the face, that saliva-swilling mouth—they came surging into his brain, driving everything else out. This Horla devil dragged him into a pit of despair so deep he couldn't feel the bottom. He kept falling, waiting for the crash that had to come.

Flogging his memory to relieve the horror, Kio clutched at the walled city of Centropolis where he had worked, where he had sweated, slept, laughed, and yes, where he had grown soft, cushioned by luxurious security. It wasn't that he was a weak man. On the contrary. His aching muscles stretched tautly over his stomach before losing themselves in the tangle of black hair and the soreness of his thighs. Those lurching muscles reflected the torchlight into the darkness from every spot where Allukah had rubbed the grease of her body into his. Yet, this wasn't just a contest of Kio pitted against the bulging sinews of the hormone-drenched Horla bitch. Till now, Kio had never had to struggle to survive. His life had been easy, too easy. His instincts were flabby, leaving him unprepared to face the part of reality men sealed out of their lives with stone walls and iron-clad laws. Allukah's world was one of blind passion, of taking anything she could grab, swallowing what tasted good and spitting out the rest. Creatures like her lived only in the instant of sensation. They were unshackled by regrets about the past, not crippled by delusions of the future. People—men like Kio—built walls to hide behind. They had to, or they became extinct. They were unprepared to meet the Allukahs. Every man was.

He should have listened to Sheryl. She knew about these things. He should have stayed where he was, in a place he knew, where he belonged. Scarcely more than a day ago, she had warned him, pleaded with him (as close to pleading as a Somelon could come). None of it had been able to convince Kio. Oh, no. He knew better. He would see for himself, make his own decisions, thank you. He would show her, show everybody, what kind of man he was.

He should have listened to her!

Again, Allukah came hemorrhaging back into his brain. He groaned, twisted, wrenched at the chains binding his hands and feet to the rock table Allukah laughed a gibbon's laugh, jumping and slapping, then she threw the cup of wine at his writhing body and she laughed some more.

The cold splash of wine on his burning skin was enough to break Kio's hysteria. He settled down on the table, his spine twitching as it touched the chilling rock. He sobbed.

Sheryl!

His thoughts raced back three weeks to that morning when he awoke, restless and unable to hold the chisel straight. He then left the studio and roamed through the swept streets of Centropolis with his head hanging, his feet kicking at the cobblestones. He smirked each time he knocked one loose, cursed when he stubbed his toe, and somewhere along the way he'd drifted into a crowd. The crowd compressed into a throng of shoving, cheering men, climbing and jumping over each other to see. Kio heard the loud, hollow hoofs of a battle charger, glimpsed the silver armor of a warrior entering the city gates with all the ecstatic welcome of a conquering hero returning from some foreign adventure. The excitement, however, failed to infect Kio. He hadn't the slightest interest in the military or politics. He was an artist, above those things. So he dropped his attention back to the cobblestones and would have turned away, but a pair of fur boots blocked his path. When he glanced up, the warrior was there in front of him, standing a full head taller than him. Their eyes locked. Kio recognized her as a Somelon immediately. He could still feel the shivers that shook him when that velvet mouth opened and she spoke to him.

"Will you come with me?"

Stunned, Kio had stuttered some kind of answer. He wasn't sure what it had been. But she took it for a consent. Picking him up off his feet, she carried him to her horse. They rode away fast, leaving the crowd behind.

Yes, he had seen desire frolicking in those green eyes, and maybe a little greed, too. Somehow that feeling didn't seem at all out of place in being there. In fact, it pleased him almost as much as it did watching her fumble with the knot in the girdle holding up his britches, the way she impatiently cursed and bit her lips, trying to unravel it, unable to contain the anticipation of what treasure she would find there. It is true that he loved her immediately. What man would not love a woman whose skin flowed over his body like warm cream, filling every eager crevice with the ripple of nerves, grasping with a feathery friction—even if it wounded his pride that she was so aggressive and he so avidly passive? Then, her father died, giving him the chance to show her exactly the kind of man he was. He taught her how to express her grief, how to rest, to depend on him. Some man! Because of him, Sheryl was dead, her beauty stiff in the dust beneath the wheels of the wagon, while he was tormented, punished for his pride by this malicious Horla demon.

"Sheryl!" Quaking with grief, Kio moaned her name.

"Sheryl?" Allukah grunted an echo and quickly jerked her 350 pounds to their full stature. Swaying only slightly as she navigated through a headful of aral-root wine, she stumbled toward him, slapping her webbed feet on the damp floor like two fat slippers.

"Sheryl?" Allukah drooled all over his chest. She bent low, seized his jaw, and forced his mouth open. Peering inside, she explored the thing that had released the name into the air.

"Sheryl?" She repeated, a bit sharper now. She was becoming impatient. "Where is she?"

Something flickered deep inside Allukah's clouded yellow eyes. Kio had seen blood-spurting rage there the night before in the wagon, when Allukah slit open the stomach of the pregnant Teutite woman who had been lying next to him. Allukah had grabbed him next, shaking him with one hand as if he were a cat, wiping the blood from her long bayonet over his pulsing Adam's apple. It was at that moment, while she was pawing him, that Kio saw the lust for blood smolder into lust for his flesh. The hunger for his body glowed in her eyes during all the sickening hours she worked over him in this cave. Until now. What had taken its place was a new mood, a volatile mixture of passion and fear coming from the depths of her instincts and tumbling around the cistern of the vacant irises of her eyes.

"Talk, white meat." Allukah poked a sharp talon between Kio's ribs. "Where's Sheryl?"

"She's dead!" Kio yelled it to make it sound like a threat. It came out like a sob.

"No!" Allukah slapped him. The blow was hard enough to loosen his molars, and it made Kio feel much better.

"Nobody can kill Sheryl. Her life belongs to me."

"You did kill her. At the wagon."

Allukah turned away from him, looking back in the direction of the caravan.

"No. I would not let it happen. No one but me."

"You did, you pig. Last night. I saw you."

Kio still saw it. He would always see it, just as he saw it that night: Sheryl bolting out of her sleep, ready to fight, leaping through the flap of the wagon. Then the club that came out of nowhere and crashed into her head. He still heard the dull, hollow sound it had made against her skull.

Kio summoned what was left of his strength and concentrated it on the tip of his tongue. When Allukah turned her coagulated face back toward him, he spit into it.

"Kill me. Go ahead. I don't care. I'd rather die than have you touch me again. Scum!"

Kio's pitiful act of defiance was enough to smother the flame in Allukah's eyes. She smiled, and the old, familiar twinkle came back. There was room for no more than one emotion at a time inside her shriveled brain. Kio's foaming saliva slid down her forehead, out onto her nose to hang suspended in a glob from its tip, until her sandpaper tongue curled out to lick it away with lingering relish.

"Not kill," she told him almost gently. Her hands started to work over his skin, kneading, probing, scraping. She swung a bristling leg across the table, mounting him as she would a horse. All the dilated pores in her sagging skin gave her the look of a giant red cinder. From out of each pore, her glands released a mixture of grease and sweat.

Kio wretched. Allukah clogged his senses completely. Her rotting breath filled up his ears. Her oily, rancid stench bored into his nose, the salty taste of her into his mouth. Kio tried to bite, tried to kick, to claw. Allukah grew more feverish with each nip, each pat, each scratch.

"There's still more man left inside you. And I want all of it!" she bellowed, then smothered out the light with her body.

Chapter 5

Shamask, the Jealous

The Sugar Desert was a colossal bald spot burned into the green scalp of the earth. Black petrified stumps stubbled its surface, hinting back to days when dewy meadows rolled where only dust devils now swirled. In the villages around its fringe, ancient, toothless mouths still croaked tales of how verdant this land had been before the Great Mushroom War. Brooks and cascades had quenched the thirst of the endless herds of elk and bison that covered the plain in a brown rug of grazing life. Massive oaks were columns supporting the sky, their branches of luxurious green ever ready to shade and cool the contented traveler. In the age before boundary walls were needed, a city had bloomed straight out of the soil, reaching higher than the oaks. That city was more fabulous, even, than Somelon, or so it was said. Things were different then, and men had the leisure to erect many stone caves, each cave having a set of eyes. They piled one atop the other, climbing upward till they clawed insolently at the stars. King and pauper alike rode wagons that needed no horse or ox to pull them. Some of these strange carts had no wheels at all, but soared through the air like eagles, winged chariots glistening above the earth. Oh, there were many fantastic stories of men and machines, of capturing the sun in bottles to hold back the night, of men who ate lightning, and of women who were made out of plastic.

But all these things had taken place before the Eight-Day Reign of Fire fused this scar into the earth's cheek. All that remained to endorse these legends was an occasional brick or rusted girder poking through the white sand like a fractured rib of some fallen giant buried in a shallow grave. The luminous Najucular stones were his shattered teeth.

Now, a lone Somelon warrior, who had never laid an eye on Somelon, raced over the dunes, sending up a feathery plume of dust in her wake. No, Sheryl hadn't outrun the dawn. Already, Shamask, the squinting sun, began to peek over her shoulder. The first handful of his rays were aimed at her golden hair. They ricocheted off, unnoticed, as did the second handful that tried to penetrate her silver helmet. Easily irritated, Shamask threw down denser, spinning waves. Each was repelled, each splashed back at him, till Sheryl's head was wrapped in a halo, and she became a nimbus gliding through the gray dawn.

Awakening from its slumber, the desert rolled over to become a swelling sea of dry surf. White waves forty feet high broke into pouring dunes that melted as soon as Sheryl tried to climb them. With each step, she slid down; with each step, she sank deeper, the loose grains swirling into whirlpools around her fur boots, drawing her in. Heated dust coated her cheeks, drizzling in between her armor to chafe her skin raw. The trail she left behind was washed away instantly—fading ripples on the surface of an ocean, as if a Somelon named Sheryl had never come within sight of this place.

Caught in sudden tides, the ground dropped away in front of her, uncovering the skeleton-littered ruins of the doomed city. Sheryl slid to a stop. Poised on the crumbling roof of a building, she didn't dare try to leap the bottomless chasms of its streets. They forced her to veer. She ran along the lengths of these archaic gorges till she found her direction again. The desert covered the city again and went after her. It wanted to drown her in its vastness, and the sun lent its radiance to the crime. But Sheryl's feet were too quick, her legs too long. She ignored them both and went on running.

The desert started to tire, but Shamask was not ready to surrender. Driven by jealousy, he pursued her. Though his heavenly aura outshone any earthly challenge, men, and women, too, shaded their eyes to admire this creature of flesh and blood, of Somelon flesh and blood, a fragile creature, whose entire life could be measured in a single eruption of his luminous gases, a trickle of his blinding light. Yet, she stole the awe that was rightly his. Yes, Shamask was jealous. Just yesterday, she had impudently stretched out that Somelon body, naked and vulnerable to the eyes of men though immune to his stream of burning ether. But that was yesterday. Today, Shamask would destroy her, even without the help of the desert. Before he would come to rest below the horizon, Sheryl would be a smoldering cinder. Shamask promised himself that much.

The higher Shamask's spiteful face rose over the horizon, the more light he sent streaking toward her. In blazing arrows, they shot over the contours of the land to strike her long, tapered neck, then her broad shoulders. Each volley struck lower than the last, glancing off the buckles that bound her armor, off the leather tongues that formed her skirt, and finally off her fur-wrapped heels. The entire rear surface of her body radiated in the heat of the morning sun. Sheryl sensed she was running deeper into trouble with each step. Out here, the only shade came when a vulture's circling body passed between you and the sun. There would be no place to hide, no way out but across the sand. She would have to keep running till she reached the other end of the desert, where there were trees, mountains to stand in front of this jealous star. There were still fifteen miles to cover.

A few beads of sweat struggled out onto her forehead. Others followed. Growing faster than the air could evaporate them, their own weight sent them plunging into her eyes. More drops followed, merging into rivulets that spread into crystal sheets. They coated her lips with the taste of salt and triggered the first hoarse cry of thirst. As the air heated, it thinned. Her breasts swelled against the steel halter, squeezing out more sweat. She was forced to breathe deeper, faster. Her lungs pulled the cascading sweat in through her nose and, as her jaw slackened, through her mouth. She coughed. She sneezed. Blinded, she stumbled. She kept on running.

Sensing a quick victory, Shamask roared out for his knights to join the battle. Bound to him by the fealty of his life-giving heat, the cold-blooded monsters squirmed out of the dunes. Their heads twitched, noses searching till Shamask's rays struck them squarely, injecting speed into their muscles, percolating their blood till they swelled and leaped. Their scales glistened on their backs like chainmail as the gila monsters snapped at Sheryl's toes. Spitting cobras aimed venomous charges at her emerald eyes. Adders twirled their slimy bodies around her legs, working their way up. But Sheryl's feet were too fast, pulling out of the gilas' jaws before they could snap. Her lids blinked away the cobras' venom. When she flexed the long muscles in her thighs, the adders snapped into pieces like leaded crystal. Incensed, Shamask surged. His rays lashed out against his own knights, driving them into a frenzied attack. Their blood began to boil, inflating their bodies, blowing them up until the pressure forced the blood out their noses, mouths, and ears.

The Somelon kept on running.

Sheryl was a warrior, but even the best of Somelons could not outrace the sun. Gradually, inexorably, heat seeped through the layers of her armor. Pressed to the inner surface of the metal, her skin shriveled, simmered slowly in its own juices, then bubbled into a sizzling steam. Refusing to let Shamask see the effect he was having on her, Sheryl kept her eyes steady, staring in front of her with her back toward him. She wanted to keep up the illusion of her immunity to him for as long as she could. She wanted to mortify Shamask, to make him feel impotent—as impotent as she was beginning to feel.

Shamask almost fell for her trick. He flared in frustration. When Sheryl felt that flux of radiation intensify, she drew renewed strength from it. Her confidence returned, knowing now that the power of a Somelon could reach into space, across the vacuum, and even squeeze the jewel of the sun.

The increased fury of Shamask's rays melted the grains of sand. They glowed white hot, splashing like molten lava, singeing the fur off Sheryl's boots. Heat rose around her like tall grass, like the slithering bodies of snakes answering the charmer's flute. The air rippled till the image of the horizon danced, a tapestry caught in a silent wind, though the only breeze in the desert was the dry whisper of Sheryl's breath. When the shimmering mirages began to close in around her, Sheryl slowed to a walk. Boldly she marched on, though she did flinch when Micar and his Horlas appeared suddenly on ponies galloping at a ghostly lope, their faces contorted into stiff, bloodless smiles. Then she felt the sword rise in her hand. It was out of its sheath, swinging, slicing through the empty air. The blade struck nothing except the sand, which spurted at the end of each stroke. The Horlas kept coming. She could hear their ponies snort, the riders yell. When the hooves of the ponies thundered over her head, when the Horlas ran right through her and disappeared, Sheryl remembered where she was and how badly she was losing the other battle, the one against the sun.

Shamask saw it, too. She was a crazy woman fighting the air. He congratulated himself on his potency, then shone still brighter.

Sheryl had squandered precious strength on mirages. Now the steel sword was hot and heavy in her limp hands. Its tip rested in the sand, she tottered around it. The human impulse to drop it tingled in her arms like a promise. But a Somelon never drops her sword as long as she has fingers to grasp it. Sheryl pulled the weapon out of the ground, slid it back into her scabbard, and trudged on.

By this time, Shamask had bobbed to his full height in the sky and began his descent to take his first peek into Sheryl's face. If he had not been there, Sheryl would have seen the fringe in front of her. But Shamask filled her eyes with his sheen, and she saw nothing else.

From this new perspective, Shamask could finally appreciate the kind of woman he was dealing with. Even as she withered, Sheryl's white skin gleamed, still immune to his scorching ultraviolet rays. Her sweat-strung hair began to dry now that her body was dehydrated and had no more extra water to pour out. The white powder coating her lips, along with her half-closed eyes, lent her a deathly beauty that softened even Shamask—but only for a moment. When he caught himself, his jealousy burst out hotter than before.

The flash blinded her. Sheryl tripped over a low brick wall jutting out of the sand and fell to the ground.

The sand embraced her, wrapping her in the folds of its hot, dry skirt. Sheryl pulled her face out, blinked empty stars, and started to crawl. In her head, the world had become a bubbling cauldron of blood, a swirling curtain of crimson fire closing in around her. She saw her father standing at its edge.

The old man's beard had grown longer, a coarse gray beard hanging between his knees, hiding the nakedness of a wrinkled body. Nervous hands floated up from his side, beckoning to her, reaching out to take her hands and pull her across into the land of the dead. The cold grave. Relief from the sun. Her words to Kryl came back to mock her, "Not as cold as the grave, old man." Sheryl reached up to her father's hands only to slap them away.

Her father's hands flew up, tearing at the air like the talons of a wounded eagle. Then Sheryl noticed the figure standing at his side.

Kio? Was he with her father now? Was this the only way she would ever see her lover again, in the land of the dead where their bodiless souls would never rub up against one another, where passion was only a dim memory diluted by infinite denial? Sheryl ran a hand over her face, down to her neck and into the front of her armor, just to feel her own flesh. It was dry, lifeless. She pulled her hand away.

Then the blade of a sword pierced the fiery curtain that now looked like cloth. Through the hole leaped Allukah. With her clouded yellow eyes glowing, she pounded on Kio, knocking him to the ground. Sheryl's father stood by, watching and smiling sweetly as Allukah trussed Kio's squirming body, dragging it back through the curtain. Her father went after him, slipping through the torn red fabric and pulling the flap closed.

"Kio!" Sheryl yelled.

She forced her body up to its knees and started to crawl, clutching at the air, the sand, pulling herself forward, chasing Allukah, chasing Kio and her father. Inch by dizzied inch, she slid over the desert floor. The red curtain disappeared to be replaced by the edge of a green carpet just a few yards away. Beyond that was the dark, oily trunk of a black-walnut tree topped with a green cap that poured out shade like a waterfall. It might all be a mirage, a last cruel trick of Shamask. When a casual breeze scooped a handful of cool mist out of the moss and threw it in Sheryl's face, she pulled herself closer.

Shamask went wild. He swelled to smother the branches of the tree. Sheryl closed her eyes, sifting her fingers through the sand till they curled around a sprout of grass with a dewdrop still trapped in its blade. Sheryl tottered, her head wheeling, her eyes rolling up inside their sockets. Her knee touched the grass. Shamask was about to burst.

Sheryl collapsed with only her hand inside the walnut's shade.

Chapter 6

The Corpse

It might have been the weight, the way its mounds and slender clefts were distributed. Or it might have been the length of the legs, the fur boots, or even the winged helmet still clinging to her head. Whatever it was, the blades of grass instantly recognized the Somelon body pressing down on them, so they reached their small green arms out of the soil to lift it. Together, they tried to raise up and slide Sheryl those last few inches into the shade. They strained so hard, the chlorophyll nearly squeezed out of their pulpy cells. Sheryl didn't budge. Shamask only shined brighter.

The blades of grass turned their small voices on the walnut tree that stood black and implacable against the sky. They pleaded, bargained, and begged, debasing themselves, till finally the majesty of its hard wood softened a trifle to dip its emerald tresses into the rays of the sun. Shade spread across the Somelon body. The blades of grass rejoiced.

Shamask still refused to give up. He was much too close to victory to let a meager, wooden-headed tree stand in his way. So the jealous star focused his flares on the walnut, dessicating the oval leaves till they shriveled brown and started to smolder. Layer after layer disintegrated as the sun's rays bore through. The full force of the sun burned closer, ever closer to that soft Somelon body so many men had coveted, the body

Shamask now wanted to reduce to ash, a burnt offering to his own, stubborn power.

The layers of leaves were too dense. There were so many of them, so many layers, one under the next. All the while Shamask raged, he kept sinking closer to the horizon. Time was slipping away for him. Desperate now, the solar general called on his allies for aid. From the east, black, grape-clustered clouds rolled across the sky, pelting the countryside with hailstones as big as grapefruits. On Shamask's blinking signal, they erupted with crackling bolts of death. Flash followed ear-blasting flash, striking the strongest branch of the walnut tree, the one directly above and shielding Sheryl. The lightning incinerated the bough. Leaves drizzled away, the bark buckled and peeled. Then the wood caught flame. Shuddering, the walnut roared in silent agony.

Then the highest mountain peak on the eastern horizon reached up to pierce Shamask's luminous cheek. Quickly, the other peaks followed, as the earth rolled its daughter out of the sun's range. Pulsing with rage, Shamask disappeared, locked below the horizon for another night.

Just as fast, the moon spread across the sky, scattering the thunderclouds. Far below, the glowing-ember wounds in the walnut's branches were a beacon, marking the spot where the Somelon's body lay still.

It was a meek sun that rose the next morning. Shamask, red faced and melting, skirted the crenelated horizon, ducking from one mountain to the next, peaking out at the Somelon body lying motionless in the moss beneath the walnut tree, before darting away.

The light woke the small animals first. Silky black

moles surfaced at Sheryl's side and floundered blindly to nuzzle against her hands. Chipmunks scurried over to nest in her hair and tangled their paws in the spun gold, chirping secrets into her ears. The deer came next, and it was the tender licking of their tongues that finally lured her back to this world.

A smile warmed on her lips when she stirred. Like the petals of a dewed morning glory, her fingers unfolded and floated up to pet the long neck of the buck, who froze at her touch. Through fluttering lids, Sheryl found the buck's ebony eyes, and in their glittering reflection she found the strength to lift her head out of the moss. The animals took a last quick look. Then, sure she would recover, they went back into the undergrowth.

She found a pool of water caught between the roots of the walnut tree. Sheryl drank, long and deep, till the water swelled into her blood, smoothing the dry folds of her skin, irrigating her hair. When she undressed to bathe, a glimpse of her Somelon body was the first reward for the valiant walnut.

Renewed by the water, Sheryl forced her eyes to look upward. They reddened when they saw that only a thin parasol of green survived on the lower branches The rest had been reduced to ash and dispersed by the wind. Worst of all was the massive branch where the lightning had struck. It clutched at the air like a cauterized artery in the muscle of a wounded warrior. This tree was as gallant as any warrior, Somelon or otherwise, Sheryl thought. It had challenged the sun and won.

Sheryl hugged the tree's trunk, kissing the rough bark. Then, taking her sword, she climbed up into the boughs. The walnut returned her caresses, helping her work her way up till her hand gripped the blackened branch. There she rested, thinking of all the years it took for this walnut to grow. They were slow years of patience, here on the foot of the desert, years of watching, of waiting, till finally she came.

Striking the base of the branch, the blade bit into wood hardened by lightning and tempered by flame. Sheryl swung at it again, then again, flicking away layer after charred layer until the wood cracked under its own weight, and the branch tumbled to the ground. Before leaping down to the grass, Sheryl ran her palm gently over the stump.

Once the smaller limbs were trimmed away, her dagger dug into the bark. It yielded eagerly, peeling away in long, hairy strips. Though fire and electricity had turned the wood to iron, when the knife started to carve, the chips flew away like so many moths set free. Sheryl carved a handle to fit her grip and notched it so that it wouldn't slip. A Somelon face was cut into the other end, a stylized portrait with coarse hair leading down to the handle and an open mouth with lips about to pucker. It was a war club, a kiss of death to be wielded by the ultimate Somelon warrior.

After the last scrawl was gouged into the wood, Sheryl hefted the weapon, holding it high above her head so the walnut tree could see it. Shamask bobbed out of hiding, and, to atone for all the mischief he'd worked, he sent down a cluster of rays to envelope the club, to light it with an incandescent blaze. This was his tribute to the walnut tree and to Sheryl. Together, they had defeated the sun. Together, they would defeat the Horlas and Allukah—and bring Kio home again.

Peeking over the crest of rocks, Sheryl saw them guarding the entrance to the cave. There were two of them, and they were only Pursangs, the toady thralls of the Horlas. On the evolutionary ladder, Pursangs were only just stretching up out of the primeval goo, reaching for the first rung. Beetle-browed and as ugly as skunks, they were incapable of acting independently, so they trailed along in the dust of the roving raiders, as jackals follow the leopard, to steal scraps of the kill and run away before getting caught. More reptile than mammal, their scaly skin hung in folds like green chainmail from their bony arms that poked out thrugh the rags they wore. Gray moss dripped out from under the earflaps of their helmets, and their hollow cheeks were smudged with grease. Their lipless mouths glistened with spittle each time their forked tongues slithered out to test the air.

Sheryl sniffed. They weren't warriors. It would be child's play to take them, hardly worth the trouble of drawing her sword. Ten yards of rocky ground stood between her and the mouth of the cave. A single cry from their shallow chests would be enough to warn Allukah and doom Kio.

So Sheryl hid, waiting for a chance. Both Pursangs were hunched over, sitting on their tails while concentrating on each throw of their bone dice. Spread out in the dirt between their knees was a brightly dyed robe, its green and red stripes serving as the board, also probably the prize in the crude contest of luck. She recognized that robe. She had bought it for Kio less than a week ago.

Sheryl had taken him to the bazaar and shamed him into trying on the gaudy garment. It clung to him almost as tightly as she did, flattering the rugged contours of his tanned muscles. There was also a long, strategically placed slit down the side that let his hairy leg peek through. It made him blush. He would have torn off the robe and stomped on it if he hadn't seen how much she liked it on him. He swallowed his pride, taking the jibes

61

of friends and strangers heaped on him, because it made her happy. Now Sheryl's happiness was spread out in the dust, cushioning the bumpy knees and feet of the slimy Pursangs. Soon, one of them would win it. One of them would drape Kio's robe over his ugly body and stick a green leg out through the slit. That shouldn't be allowed to happen.

It was then that Sheryl felt the cold tip of a sword press into the back of her neck. Slowly, carefully, she turned her head to see the huge, scaly paw perching on her shoulder.

"I knew if I waited long enough the great god Shamask would reward me." Sticky breath hissed into her ear. It was heavy with the smell of onions—old, fermented onions.

Sheryl's swordbelt was cut away, then one by one the straps holding her armor in place. The steel breastplate clattered over the rocks, leaving her protected by only a thin chemise.

"Turn around and let me take a gander at the prize the sun awards his faithful, long-suffering servants."

Obeying the voice, Sheryl discovered it came from the throat of a creature very large for a Pursang. His head was a bulb of leathery fat with no real nose, just two small craters in the center of his face. A scar trickled down from his sloping forehead to his cheek, sealing one eye closed. Every few seconds, a thin, gassy flame flickered out of his mouth, along with a pink, forked tongue. His beard was a tangle of seaweed glistening over a flaccid chest that bulged against a burlap jerkin. At a glance, Sheryl saw she could crush him bare-handed. But without the instant death sealed in the blade of her sword, he would have time to cry out, to warn the others—and Allukah.

"You sure are a nice one," the Pursang slobbered,

scanning over the things that made her a woman, dwelling on the things that made her a Somelon. "And big. Yes, sir. I like big women."

"Please, oh, please." Sheryl pleaded in her highest-pitched voice. "Take whatever you want from me. I give it gladly. Just tell me if you've seen my poor husband. Two nights ago, the Horlas stole him from my bed. I've taken his sword and his armor in the desperate hope that I can find him. But what can I, a helpless woman, do against the strength of men, especially the strength of Pursangs? Oh, please. You've got to help me."

"Too bad, lady. If he's the one Allukah's got in there, you'll get nothing back but a bloodless carcass. She drains 'em like a cask of aral-root wine, then smashes the empties against the rocks."

"Oh, please. Won't you look for me? I'll reward you. I'll reward you better than you've ever known."

"Reward me? Sure. But rewards first." His free claw reached out to pinch her cheek.

"Natoo!"

The call came from the cave. Sheryl cringed, praying Allukah wouldn't hear it. The big Pursang turned to wave wildly at the dice players. He didn't want Allukah to hear either.

"Quiet, you fools!" Natoo spit through rocky teeth, then shrugged to his captive. "Let's go."

The sword rested in the sling formed by the straps of her chemise, digging into the skin of her back as she climbed over the low wall of boulders. Still kneeling on Kio's robe, the other two Pursangs froze with their mouths gaping when they saw this seven-foot apparition tiptoe over the tacks in their direction, her breasts peaking out of her short chemise. Puffing small clouds of dragon smoke, they scrambled to their feet, claws extended, clutching, clicking like castanets. Natoo stopped them with a stare.

"She's not for sharing. You two can watch, maybe. That oughta be enough for scrawny worms."

Their sudden hopes suddenly shattered, the two smaller Pursangs drew back, hissing, glutting their tiny brains with atrocities against Natoo that they dared not carry out. They would save the best ones, just in case they ever got the chance to put them into practice.

"No need to squabble, boys." Sheryl fluttered her eyelids coyly. "There's enough here for all of you."

A flick of her hand took one strap of the chemise off her shoulder. Then she smiled as she peeled the other away. The sheer fabric slid down till it caught on the tips of her breasts, lingered there for an eternal instant, before it floated to the ground, leaving Sheryl standing there before their flinching eyes with only fur boots protecting her smooth, white body. Stepping out of the pool of fabric, she pirouetted.

Her breasts looked like melting snow cones topped with cherries. Beneath them, the taut muscles of her stomach twitched, ready to wriggle. Her fluted back tapered down before flaring out into her hips. From there down, she was all legs, long, slender legs that could wrap around a man's neck and smother him in pleasure.

"My God!" one of the small Pursangs said, nearly choking on his own smoke.

"A goddess," quivered the other, shielding his eyes from the radiance of the sight.

"A man could get lost in there and never be heard from again!"

"*Three* men," Sheryl purred.

His greed as overstimulated as his gonads, Natoo refused to yield. A flaming tongue flicked out a warning.

"She's mine," he roared, taking her arm and lifting the tip of his sword to their faces.

"Come on." Sheryl stretched toward him, letting them all see more of her. "How can you enjoy yourself with these two buzzing around you like dung flies? I can take the three of you. At once."

"No!" Natoo shook.

"Oh, put away your weapon, warrior." Sheryl gently pushed the heavy blade down. "You don't need a sword to protect yourself from me, unless you're afraid I'm too much woman for you. Not a steel sword, anyway. All you need is that other sword hiding under your britches."

Natoo stared at her, his reptilian senses too coarse to absorb this barrage of sensuality in one gulp. The sword settled down, while his free, chicken-footed hand rose up to pause at her breast before settling in her hair.

"Yes, Natoo. Let my golden hair tickle your strong hand. Run your fingers through it." Sheryl led the sword back into its sheath.

"A man is all sword—to a woman." Her warm, naked body wrapped around him like a cloud of steam, letting the scented vapor rise into the holes in his face where a nose should have been. She ran her palm down his chest until it reached the sword and stroked its handle. "Long, stiff, thrusting deep into the core of a woman, pumping the ultimate pleasure into her."

With her fingertips, she eased the weapon an inch out of its sheath. Natoo stiffened instinctively, but he relaxed as soon as she licked her lips and let the sword slide back into the sheath under its own weight. Behind her, Sheryl heard the other two Pursangs whimpering. She wiggled. They started to cry.

"A real man teases a woman with his sword," Sheryl

went on, pouting. "He knows how much she needs it, so he tickles her with it, drawing it out slowly, then plunging it back in."

In time with her words, Sheryl's hand toyed with the sword, sliding it out, then slamming it back into the scabbard.

Natoo felt twinges of pleasure crawling over his fat body every time the sword jiggled and her hand rubbed over the shining ball that tipped the pommel. His eyes began to close, enjoying this foreplay as much as a cat having its belly scratched. The other Pursangs could do nothing but drool, as their cold, thick blood sputtered through their veins like jellied gasoline.

"A woman moans. 'Faster,' she cries. 'More sword. More sword! Deeper. Deeper. Please, my angel. Cut me. Cut me, please!' She trembles, grabs for the sword. Wild now, she forces it all the way inside her. Then she pulls it *out!*"

With a muffled cry, Sheryl ripped the sword into the air and sank it into the skull of the fat Pursang. After the initial thud, when it cleaved bone, the blade made no more than a whisper as it sliced down through his chest all the way to his crotch, splitting him in two. The halves hung there for an instant, propped against one another as the green blood, the spongy brown lungs, the liver and intestines sloshed out into the sand. Then the halves toppled over, limp.

Sheryl turned on the other two Pursangs, who were clutching at each other as their lust crystalized into cold fear. When they opened their mouths, instead of flames, only puffs of thin smoke came out. Sheryl skewered them both, ending their fear forever.

Standing over the still-quivering bodies, her lips curled up over her pearly teeth. "Pursangs," she sneered, wiping the sword in the purifying sand. Then she sliced off the braid of hair the fat Pursang had contaminated and threw it to one half of his carcass.

"Fight with yourself over this."

Sheryl stooped over to gather Kio's robe in her arms. The bone dice scattered, coming up with three eights showing on their faces.

"Boxcars. You lose, fellas."

Sheryl turned and stalked off to fetch her armor.

The steel door that once reached twenty feet overhead to seal the mouth of the Jibway caves had long since rusted away and now was little more than a reddish-brown stain across the rock floor. Just past the entrance, tunnels and corridors shot out in all directions, dissolving into impenetrable darkness. Jibway was a colossal hive carved into solid granite by some long-extinct bees. Sheryl was ready to poke her nose into every one of its cells if it meant finding Allukah— and poor Kio, of course.

The first passage she chose was garlanded with shining strands of film that rustled in the light of Sheryl's torch, curling into sudden flames when the torch strayed too close. More piles of film, glossy and tangled as the hair of some synthetic sea monster, crackled under the soles of her boots. On all sides, the walls were tiled with brass plates, each one inscribed with words of a language so old even the Somelons had forgotten it. The deeper she penetrated, the more plates she found. Some of them had been pried out away from the wall; they weren't plates at all, but drawers, each crammed with spools of the ebony film. These were the secrets of the ancient ones. Drawers upon drawer, row upon row, bursting with data well-preserved that no living brain could decipher. They would become that much tickertape, so much bunting for looters—Horlas, and Pursangs. No, Sheryl didn't know what microfilm was, except that its fragile, crisp sheen was treasured by merchants and harlots alike. At that moment, she had more on her mind than cheap trinkets.

Sheryl chose just as badly the second time. This tunnel had already been stripped of its drawers. Instead, rows of bamboo cages lined both walls. On their matted floors were scattered a few handfuls of filth-choked straw, all the comfort Allukah's human pets could ever expect. The cages were empty now, though the gnawed bars, the clots of blood and hair hinted at the atrocities that had echoed through these dark alleys.

At the farthest end of the third tunnel, Sheryl spied a dim light. Discarding the torch, she raced toward the glow, her feet padding soundlessly over the slippery rocks as she hugged the dripping walls. Stopping just before the alley curved, Sheryl peeked around the bend.

She found a great vault with a ceiling that rose far out of reach of the smoldering torch thrust into the limestone wall. There was more than enough light to see the stone table in the center of the room.

Sheryl didn't find Allukah waiting for her in that vault. The Horla witch had fled, perhaps warned by the cries of the Pursangs, or maybe because she had simply glutted her subhuman hunger and moved on.

Sheryl didn't find Allukah, but chained to the stone table she found the shriveled body Allukah had milked dry. He was slit open, his dead eyes still searching for the ceiling they would never find.

Chapter 7

Between Two Worlds

With clouds masking the moon, the night was as thick as grease. The only light seen winked out of zigzagging Najucular stones, as spraying cobras scooped them into their mouths to tempt fireflies to their doom.

The yoke lashed to his shoulders, along with the weight of the crate on his back, forced Kio's head down so that all he could see were the white blurs of his bare toes flicking out from under the purple robe with each trudging step. But Kio didn't have to see where he was going. There was a horsehair noose looped tightly around his neck, always pulling him in the right direction. The direction wasn't right because it led to one place in particular. No, it was right because it led away from strangulation.

She had chosen to let Kio live, for the moment, though he had to watch while Allukah chained a tearful Teutite groom to the stone table and split open his belly. His intestines squirmed out of him, and the groom didn't die then, not right away. He had probably known she planned to kill him, though he couldn't have predicted just how. Still, when it happened, his eyes overflowed with surprise, and they locked on Kio's, asking him silently, "Why?"

Kio never tried to answer. Free of his bonds, he might have grabbed for Allukah's hand before the dagger sliced through the boy. It wasn't likely he would have stopped her, but he might have tried. Or he might have run away instead, out of the cave, ran after his own life. But Kio did none of these things. He did nothing. He felt nothing. He just watched the groom die, because that's where his eyes happened to be looking at the time.

When the spasms of the groom passed into history, Allukah turned to Kio with a broad smile. She wiped her bloody hands over his face, forcing her crooked fingers into his mouth. Kio bit them, grinding his bare teeth together till his gums and jaw ached, till Allukah's blood mixed with the blood of the groom and choked Kio. A foot in his stomach and a kick in the head were all it took to free Allukah's hand and make her happy again.

"You're holding out on me, pet. There's still more man left in you. I want it—all of it."

With that, she took him one last time. Amid the slobbering, the groaning, and the suffocating weight of her fat body, Kio discovered a change had come over him. His revulsion had vanished. So did the shame. He lay there on the cold, hard floor, detached and limp, as if it weren't really his flesh, as if it were all a story he had heard somewhere, long ago, a long story that wasn't unusually interesting. Kio was mildly gratified. His nerves had been so abused, so overloaded, that now they simply refused to stir. Exhausted, they had gone to sleep. Harassed, they had fallen into a coma.

Even when Allukah, disappointed with his poor performance, grabbed for her bullwhip, Kio didn't flinch. The crack of the lash was just another sound. The red zebra stripes cut into his back were just another sensation. Cold, hot, hard, soft—those were tangible, feelable. Pleasure, pain, good, bad—only words whose meaning Kio had forgotten.

"You're as cold as a snail and twice as soft," Allukah cursed him in disgust. Then she heard something far away, at the mouth of the cave, Pursangs yelling to each other in their lizardy voices. That was when she turned Kio into a beast of burden to carry her plunder from the raid on the Teutite caravan. Besides Kio, she had taken only the armor and tools of Sheryl's parents. Lashing the crate to his back, she yoked him, and they fled the echoing ring of voices, coming out on the opposite side of the mountain.

As he trudged along through the dusty night behind the tail-swished flanks of Allukah's speckled gelding, Kio was sure there wasn't a trace of a man left anywhere inside him. The deepest recess of his mind had been exposed, the last reserve of his strength drained, and the smallest hidden cavity of his self-respect scraped as clean as the belly of that Teutite groom.

When his foot became tangled in the ragged hem of his robe, Kio tripped. The weight of the crate on his back pushed him down hard, grinding that once-handsome face into the gravel, but the leash caught him before he reached the ground, jerking his head up with a snap. His eyes bulged. The noose pulled tighter, sealing the dry breath inside his lungs. There was an instant of raw panic. Then he surrendered.

Calm again, Kio's mind took a few steps outside his festering body and looked down at the scene. He watched the noose drag him along, with the edge of the yoke digging into the ground like a weird plow. A few short minutes without air, and it would all be over. What did it matter? Sheryl had been dead for two days, and by now the jackals had turned her into their own flesh and blood. There wasn't anybody else in this desolate world who could care one way or the other—and that included Kio. In a few short minutes, his skin would turn as blue as a Boroka nomad. In a few more, he would be where Sheryl was, leaving this worn-out

71

body behind, just as a snake slides out of its skin or a snail from its shell. Kio was about to molt into another life. Better yet, he might even find oblivion waiting.

It took only a rock in the path to spoil these luscious dreams. When the yoke struck it, Kio flipped over. The noose snapped at his neck again with such force it almost jerked the dozing Allukah out of her saddle. She pulled at the reins, and the noose slackened. When he hit the ground, Kio's mind plunged back into his body.

While he rocked on his back as helpless as a turtle, the figure of Kio's master stood between him and the unmasked moon. Her head was tipped with a spiked helmet; below, a breeze rustled through her coat, lifting up the different-colored pelts to show the pulpy, pocked flesh Kio knew too well. Allukah's coat was a loose patchwork of blond, red, and green mousy hair of Pursangs, scalps of all the men who had serviced her. Each divot had been ripped from their freshly smashed skulls like so much sod from red clay. There were enough scalps to reach as far as Allukah's hob-nailed boots, almost covering their brass spurs. It was only one of her many coats.

"You can't lay down yet. It's not time for you to die." Her voice was an avalanche of sound crashing into Kio's head. "I'll let you know when it is. Now up, mule! There are miles to go before you can rest."

She reached out with one hand and lifted Kio off the ground, to hold him dangling in the air. When she lowered him back down, his leg joints locked, and Kio stood there tottering.

"I had to teach you how to service a woman, and you certainly weren't a star pupil. Do I have to teach you to walk now?"

Kio didn't even bother to look at her. He kept his parched tongue safely in his mouth, his eyes on the ground.

"Sulking won't do you any good, you know. I don't care for it." Allukah's eyes were two smoldering, smoking volcanoes. "Maybe you're thirsty. Is that what's making you so cranky?"

As Allukah unlaced the waterbag from the saddle, Kio's eyes bobbed up like corks on a yellow sea. He watched every move as she held it to her purple lips. The clear, cool liquid splashed into the great cavity of her mouth, filling it, overflowing in long, silvery streams to mat the scalps on her coat. Then she licked herself with her sandpaper tongue.

"Care for a swig?" she gurgled. "Well, maybe if you dance for me, I'll give you a swig."

Kio puckered to spit his answer. There wasn't enough saliva in his mouth to drown a flea.

"Dance, mule." Allukah drank again. "Aren't you thirsty? I sure am."

As if with a mind of their own, his blistered, torn feet began to move. Rising to his toes, Kio danced. The yoke held his arms out from his body to make him look like some ugly, featherless nestling with splinted wings. The crate bounced on his neck, cutting into his shoulders. Kio danced, circling at the end of the leash, beating his shredded feet into the ground, bending, shaking till Allukah made him stop.

"Enough. Enough already. You dance with all the grace of a ruptured mule." Contemptuously, she poured the water into the sand. "I'm sorry, but I don't seem to have a silver cup handy, and I know you wouldn't want to drink out of the same bottle as me. Would you? Can't be too careful with one's health."

Just like a nestling on its first flight, Kio swooped down to the ground, plunging his face into the puddle of mud between Allukah's boots. He tried to lap up the

73

water with his tongue before it seeped into the earth. When it disappeared into the sand, he went after it, filling his mouth with mud, squeezing it dry, then spitting out the grains. Kio dove in for more, digging with his nose, scratching with his chin.

Allukah chuckled lightly, but the diversion was already wearing thin. Mounting the gelding, she dug her spurs into its flanks. When it leaped forward, it pulled Kio's head out of the hole in the sand.

The Pursangs had taken Kio's clothes after Allukah stripped them off his back. While he was chained to the table for her instant pleasure, it was much more convenient to keep him naked, with every part of him accessible to her whims. Yet, outside the cave, he needed something to cover him, if only because Allukah had so quickly tired of looking at him, so she had thrown him a purple robe.

"To match your bruised thighs," she told him, "and the pulpy mass hanging between them."

The nap of thick material was worn down to a shine, it was stained with the blood and sweat of the men or apes who had serviced Allukah before she found Kio. The robe hung as stiff as cardboard over his limbs, extending a few inches longer than his legs, making each step he took an awkward contest of skill and precision. It was a contest Kio lost as often as he won. When he lost, he stumbled again, to be dragged by the neck across the rocky ground.

As Kio shuffled along, the aching orbs between his legs slapped from one thigh to the next, swinging like pendulums. The entire foreskin was gone from his penis, shredded by Allukah's coarse hair, coarsened by her two sets of chapped lips, and gnawed by her crooked teeth. She had drained all the juices out of his body, leaving him a husk, without the strength to dream or the

74

need to think. All of Kio's ego was gone. The energy, the creativity that had coaxed iron, wood, and marble into becoming goddesses and cherubim now belonged to Allukah. Kio was bare on the inside, like a pig's bladder, swollen and hard, with nothing to support it but air. What was left of him hovered between two worlds: Torn out of civilization and plunged into unrelieved chaos, he could accept neither. Unable to trust thought or feeling, Kio was willing to survive only if it wasn't going to be too much trouble.

They had been on the road since sundown, racing between shelters. Allukah roamed only at night. During the journey, they didn't have time to eat or rest. They stopped only when Allukah went out to gather more of the luminous Najucular stones she popped into her mouth like cashews.

"I don't fear the sun, you understand." Allukah had to raise her voice to cut through the sound of the horse's hoofs. She wanted Kio to hear; though he was a slave, she couldn't bear for him to get the wrong idea about her.

"Allukah fears nothing, but Shamask is my enemy. It's only to his advantage if I'm caught out in the open, on his ground, on his terms. Look at what he's done to me already." Allukah gulped another glowing stone.

"Yes, I'm ugly. No one has to say it. Yet, there was a time you would have stood in line to hear my voice, when you'd have sold your pretty little soul for a glimpse of my slim ankles. Oh, yes," she belched, "my skin was the whitest, the smoothest, my hair the blondest the world had ever seen."

Her cloudy eyes scanned the darkness as though she could still see it all happening: the kings and princes preening, the jealous, catty hissing of courtesans and queens.

"I was perfect till that spiteful star attacked me with all its force when I was weakest. Shamask dried out my skin. He shriveled my body into a cinder. If it wasn't for the Najucular stones," she said, popping another gem into her mouth, "I probably would have died. They alone preserve me, light me from within with light as bright as Shamask's. My strength has never left me, and now I'm on the road back. I've stretched my skin with fat to even out the wrinkles. With the help of the Najucular stones, my skin, then my hair will glow again. Soon! Very soon. I'll be beautiful again. Men will kill one another for the honor of kissing my toes. They'll climb mountains just to look down the neck of my dress. I'll be a goddess again, with centaurs to serve me. I'll meet Shamask face to face, and we'll see who's stronger."

She pounded the neck of her horse. It whinnied, twisting its head to snap its teeth at her fingers, though it knew better than to bite her.

"Till then, I'll be queen of the night."

Allukah went silent after that, content to sit in the saddle, stuffing one stone after another down her throat. Before Kio's moonlit eyes, she seemed to grow fatter. The dark smudge over her upper lip filled out to become a thick mustache.

The further they traveled, the more the silhouettes on the landscape altered, melting from high, rocky crags infested with scroll-horned rams, into a dry, lifeless tundra. On either side of the waterless riverbed they followed, gray grass lay in tangled balls, the mounds piling atop one another like dirty cotton. The sharp rock and crumbling clods had been left behind, but new obstacles threatened Kio. Lying just beneath the smooth surface of the dusty aqueduct channeling them through the night were plastic sheets, broken bottles, and empty cans. He kept stubbing his toes on shards of sharp glass that spurted out, glistening in the reflected light of the Najucular stones. Large aluminum cans also formed hidden snares. Every time he stepped on one, it hissed, as the air, trapped inside for decades, rushed out and the metal collapsed with a crinkling clap. The sharp, jagged corners of the cans tore at Kio's bare feet like the hungry mouth of a flesh-eating fish suddenly awakened from hibernation. Kio lurched forward, and the cans bit into his shins, his knees, before a quick tug of the leash in Allukah's hand turned a simple stumble into a complete fall. The cans took a turn at his chest, his face, tearing out little bits of him, till somehow he struggled back to his feet. All the while, Allukah's pie-footed gelding plodded on without missing a hoofbeat.

As the darkness congealed, featherless wings swam through the heavy air, some settling on the edge of the crate strapped to Kio's back. Perching like mutant parrots, the bats peered down at the bowed head of their porter. Discussing the situation in high-pitched, squealing gossip, their little mouths flashed thorny teeth. It wasn't long before one of them dared to hop down to the yoke. Leaning over Kio's sweating head, it tugged at his hair and nibbled his ear. When Kio did nothing, the others hopped down to join in. Soon, one had the courage to bite, injecting his fangs into Kio's neck. He screamed.

"Quiet!" Allukah turned in the saddle. Her whip reached out, licking a welt into Kio's forehead. "We're getting near the camp, and I don't want you to wake them all up. It'll be less trouble for both of us if we sneak in without being seen."

Squirming, twisting, Kio tried to shake off the vermin gnawing at his neck. His arms strained against the thongs, holding him in the yoke, but he couldn't even come close to reaching the black little body. It hung there suspended only by its mouth, sucking Kio's blood into its gullet, its belly swelling into a furry balloon. Another bat dropped down, tangling its claws in Kio's scalp and rearing back for its bite. Kio screamed.

Allukah's whip lashed out again. Then a whistle on the wind crystalized into an arrow that impaled the sucking vampire to the yoke. The furry balloon burst, splattering Kio's face and neck with hot, black blood— Kio's own blood, contaminated and clotting. The other bats scattered.

There was a laugh, a tinkle of bells in the night, then another shaft slammed into the yoke just above Kio's head.

Chapter 8

In the Great Hut

Allukah wrenched back the reins of her gelding. The noose around Kio's neck slackened. He choked when he breathed in a full breath of air laced with his own blood.

Driving a hand deep into the leather bag laced to her saddle, the Horla Queen pulled out fire and held it high over her head. A few yards to the right, sitting cross-legged on top of a boulder, was a giggling, misshapen creature with a hairy face crowned by a garland of poison oak. An eyepatch had shifted over his nose. It was Maskim, the cretin son of the maiden Cranulia, who they say died of fright when she saw the kind of creature that had been hiding in her belly for eleven months. A crossbow still vibrated in Maskim's pudgy hands.

"Put out that light, Allukah," the cretin said, shielding his sloping brow. "The night is kind to our poor eyes. It hides your ugly face, so we only have to hold our noses to keep from smelling your stench that gets there an hour before you do. But hold on. What's that on the end of your leash?"

Maskim scrambled up to his short legs, though they made him no taller than when he was sitting. Tiny bells tinkled inside his sheepskin cape.

"Why, he's almost as ugly as you. Better let me put a shaft through his heart. Quick, before somebody else sees him and you lose your place in the ugly hall of fame."

"My little donkey here will show you up for the imbecile you are, Maskim. Even he knows that only rotten fruit ever oozed out of Cranulia's festered womb."

She was close enough to see his lower lip sag down from his broken teeth. The upper lip rolled back as high as his flaring nostrils. The crossbow toppled from his hand.

"And what comes out of your womb, Allukah? Old boots, candelabras, anchors, and goalposts. There isn't a male gopher between here and Somelon that would get within six miles of you if you didn't sink your claws into his neck and force him to get it up. If you had the strength of only a normal woman, you would have to satisfy your goatish appetite with broom handles and sword pommels—not that you're a stranger to them now. Every stick, every tapered rock, even cactuses quiver when they see you coming. You go around sticking things inside you as if you were looking for the key to a lock. Well, your lock's rusted, Allukah. The only way to open it is to split it in two."

"Maskim, you're a crippled dog who doesn't know his own father, so you go from man to man, sniffing between their legs, hoping you'll recognize the scent."

"And most of the time what I find is your sickening smell—at least, when the men are grizzly baboons and as weak as snails. Most men would rather stuff a turkey, and a tom turkey at that, before being desperate enough to touch you, moldface."

"You're just a blooksucking flea, cretin. Why don't you try my horse's rump? My hide's too thick for your pinchers."

Allukah's whole body shimmied in delight. She enjoyed trading insults with the halfwit—as long as she could keep it under control.

"Not as thick as the bones in your head. Or the saddlehorn between your legs." He shifted from one foot to the other, ready to jump at the first sign of Allukah's anger. "But you are famous. I'll have to give you that. From one horizon to the next, men throw up at the mention of your name. Yes, like buzzards. Like sea anemones, they throw up their guts in fear, fear they might have to look at your pebbly face, as though that fly-bait body of yours, with breasts like hanging cakes of fungus, weren't enough to put a man's stomach in his mouth. In my time, I've seen men who had been hit with the ugly stick—cretins, like me, hunchbacks, dwarfs, and sailors, men locked in the bodies of animals or slugs. But you, Allukah, you *swallowed* that ugly stick, and it wasn't with your mouth. Ugliness is your vocation. You take to it like a rat to garbage—naturally."

"Oh, Maskim. You have such a way with words." Allukah leaned back, curling one leg over the saddle. "You make me laugh. Not many can."

"All you need is a mirror, my sweet. If that doesn't make you laugh, you're dead."

"But you're such a coward. You nip and run, afraid to stand your ground."

"I hold my water, not my ground, dung face. I may be a cretin, but I'm not a fool who would get close enough to a pig whose father was cockroach spit, a rotten sow whose breasts feed her children blood instead of milk."

"Because of those breasts, my son will rule the Horlas, then the world."

"Your son? I've got your son right here." Maskim jiggled his crotch. "But what about your daughter, Allukah?"

As if a spur had dug into its side, the gelding reared,

81

almost throwing Allukah from the saddle. She fought to hold on, yelling as she did, "My daughter's dead."

"Wishful thinking." Maskim clapped his hands, his little feet dancing as he watched her. "Suppose I told you I've seen her. Suppose I tell you I've talked to her, that she told me how much she wants to see you again, to make up for old times. Suppose," he held up a crooked finger, squinting over it as if it were the sight on the end of his crossbow, "suppose I tell you I've fixed it for her—a family reunion?"

Before the last word left his mouth, an unseen tongue flashed out through the air, snapping the outstretched finger off at the joint. Quick as a cobra, the bullwhip cracked again, curling round the place where Maskim's neck should have been. It wrenched the squat body forward.

"You're lying now. And I stopped laughing."

Foaming acid suddenly drenched Allukah's voice as she reeled him in. Maskim tried to work the stubby fingers that remained on his hand in between the whip's leather coils and his throat, but Allukah dragged him under the gelding's hoofs, then dismounted to kick him.

Kio leaned against the side of the riverbank, content to see someone else bear the brunt of the distorted passions he had endured so long.

"There are things you will learn not to talk about."

Allukah buried the tip of her hobnailed boot in the cretin's chest. Maskim squealed.

"Not even in jest."

Allukah turned to Kio. She winked, and a mischievous smile played on her hairy lips, but she directed her voice to Maskim. "You didn't like the looks of my pet. You might be right. The poor thing's tired. Look at the way he struggles under the weight of his load. He deserves a rest, don't you think?"

She uncoiled the whip and drew it back, ready to strike.

"I'm talking to you, cretin."

"Yes," Maskim hid between the horse's legs, a monkey in a cage. "By all means. Give him a rest."

"Good." She twitched her arm, and the whip kissed Maskim again, though lightly, just enough to make sure he wouldn't forget.

When the journey started again, there were three of them headed for the Horla village. Allukah led the way, seated backward on the gelding so that she could gloat and bounce Najucular stones off Maskim's sloping forehead. The cretin shuffled along behind, his skull dented by her boots, his hand bleeding where there had recently been a finger, and his hunched back bowed even lower under the weight of the crate. Kio brought up the rear. Freed of his load, though still yoked and leashed, he fell one more time before they reached the village gate.

Built atop a massive mound jutting out of the plain, the Horla camp was a collection of mud huts, small, smoky ziggurats swelling out of the heap like pimples on the jaw of an old Mahomite whore; the sparse weeds between the huts were like hair growing out of her moles. The gate to the village was an arch twenty feet tall, decorated randomly with Horla booty. Brass monkeys scrambled over it, their tails dangling. Hubcaps reflected the firelight like so many rusted mirrors. It was all held together by woven strands of insulation wire.

Circling out from both sides of the doorless gate was a low wall of wooden staves, full of gaps and fallen sections. There was no need to keep it in repair, for only Somelons dared attack Horlas, and Somelons had long since retreated to wherever Somelons go. Anyway, if a Somelon did want to get in, she wouldn't be stopped by a mere wall, not even if that wall were made of concrete and invar. Nobody else in this world would think of entering the camp—willingly.

The location of the village had been carefully selected for the rich deposits lying just beneath the surface. A casual scratch in this loose dirt would uncover an aluminum can, or maybe a sacred plastic talisman formed into six loops in honor of the six original Horla gods: Jor, Aah, Sett, Faut, Mae, and the bloody Fer. Crumbling rubber foamed under foot, and green plastic cabbages sprouted. Flies were everywhere, so many that they filled the Horla's bread as if they were raisins.

Normal people would have mined the mound and stripped it of all of its loot. Yet, Horlas, as everyone knew, were not normal people. Their imagination was thin, blanketed by a thick layer of dizziness. What's more, the ground wasn't much of a challenge. It just laid there, never putting up a fight when you robbed it, never bleeding when you stabbed it, or screaming when you tore it apart. No, thank you. Horlas would rather fight. They would rather die than be reduced to digging in the ground like worms.

All told, there were nine concentric, diamond-shaped tiers of ziggurats on the mound surrounding the Great Hut. If the ziggurats were pimples, the Great Hut was a giant carbuncle pushing up out of a festering wound. That was where Allukah was headed.

It must have been Maskim's croaking that alerted the Horlas. As soon as the three pilgrims passed under the gate and set foot inside the first tier, naked children and pregnant women poured into the narrow streets like ants out of an anthill. The naked boys and girls looked like pipe-limbed, globe-bellied pygmies with matted hair

84

dangling into their black eyes and bloated ticks hanging from their necks. Their mothers were infected harpies wrapped in the remnants of exotic robes. Whether dyed silk, brocades, or silver-threaded or piped with gold, the clothes were plundered by the men from under-guarded caravans. Never washed, never changed, the once-fine, delicate garments meant for princesses and queens, hung from the Horla women like autumn leaves from fat trees.

The crowd cheered Allukah, choking the streets until her gelding had to step over their bodies or knock them out of the way with its sharp hoofs. Their screams were lost in the cheers. Maskim was encircled and pelted with stones by tiny Horlas, who stayed just beyond the reach of his short arms. The children were even more curious about the new target at the end of the noose, the one with its broken wings lashed to the yoke.

The strange beast captured their weak imaginations. Sure, it walked on its hind legs like a Horla or a bear, but there were ten full fingers on its smooth hands, and the only fur on its white body grew out in curls from its scalp. The skin was as unblemished as a newborn lamb, except where those purple blotches made it look like a leopard's pelt. There was also that bat tacked by an arrow to the wood on the side of his head. Also, the beast moaned so queerly when they struck it. No, it couldn't be a bear. And it couldn't be a Horla. So they explored the beast, probing it with sharp sticks, scattering when it bellowed.

The second time they pierced the beast's hide, they ran only a few feet away before regrouping and tiptoeing back. Inspired by the familiar red drops that started to leak from the wounds, they surrounded him, giggling, encouraged by mothers proud of their little warriors. They pulled bones and glass out of the ground, as well as angry embers from the campfires, and flung them in Kio's face, clapping and dancing when a hot coal lodged between the yoke and his shoulder, sending the beast into a blind rage.

Kio spun, trying to dislodge the ember burning through his skin. He squirmed away from the point of one stick, only to drive himself into another. Swerving and dipping the yoke through the air, he sent small bodies flying. More sticks came out to fill the ranks, jabbing, slicing through his robe, shredding his skin. One stick slid between his feet. He fell, dragged along by the neck. Tiny hands ripped away his robe, clawed at his face, and his genitals became the prime target of the sharp sticks. That's when consciousness thoughtfully abandoned his brain.

The fun went out of it then. Torturing a limp hunk of flesh that didn't scream or resist was pretty lame entertainment, even for a young Horla. So when Allukah rode into the ninth tier and reined her horse in front of the Great Hut, mothers quickly pulled their children away, though they did take the impaled bat with them for their supper.

Where she came from, Kio would never know. But the gentle pressure of a cool rag against his face snapped open his eyes and there she was, kneeling over him. She was a slightly built woman with a small, round mouth and the bottomless black eyes of a fawn. Maybe it was only a trick of his twisted, swollen brain the way her translucent skin seemed to glow from within, as though a lantern was hidden inside her. Yet even in the dim light of the Horla village he captured every feature of her tender face that was outlined by the fur of the hood covering her head. A damp linen cloth draped over her outstretched hands. With it she wiped his face clean, carefully, letting the magnetic coolness linger as she eased him back to consciousness. Kio watched as the grime from his cheeks stained the linen with a melting caricature of his face.

Then the light blinked out inside her as Allukah loomed over them. When the Horla queen snatched the woman away, Kio went after her. But the leash pulled him back down and the yoke kept him floundering.

Allukah flipped the little woman up. Spinning off into the darkness, she made only a tiny squeal when she hit the ground. Then Kio was alone again, until that paw reached out for him.

Pulled to his feet and propped against the wall of the Great Hut, Kio was stiff as one of the scarecrows working the day shift in a Poloma cornfield. He scanned the village. There was no sign of the woman with the linen cloth and glowing skin.

As soon as Allukah released Maskim, he scrambled out of her reach, before turning to taunt her.

"I owe you for this, you rat-faced sow."

"It was my pleasure." Allukah laughed.

"And my pleasure's about to come," Maskim screamed rubbing his hump where the crate had bruised it. "I'll bring somebody around to see you. Somebody who'll cut those cloudy eyes right out of your fat head."

With that, Maskim dove into the ring of huts looking for a child to steal, a dog to kick. Allukah shrugged and drew the dagger out of her belt, then turned back to Kio.

"Don't think I've forgotten you, my pet." The knife sparkled, a silver fang ready to inject death into Kio's veins. "All the fight's gone out of you. Even children are too much for you to handle. I guess there's only one thing left to do to you."

Kio leaned forward, just a trifle, fighting every muscle in his body that wanted to shrink back. The blade offered a quick, lasting relief from this torture. Standing on blistered feet, he swayed, waiting for the tooth to bite.

"You come to me like a greedy child after a gift." She grazed his throat, driving shivers down his spine with the icy dagger. Kio pressed his neck to the point and Allukah quickly pulled it away, only scratching him slightly. The silver fang nibbled at his shoulder, slid up along his arms to slice through the leather thongs. The yoke crashed to the ground.

Splinted for so long at right angles to his body, Kio's arms stayed locked. The shreds of the purple robe dripped away like the petals of a wilted lilac.

"Did you enjoy the welcome my people gave you? They want you to stay, and who am I to disappoint them? I think I'll give you to the children. They'd like that. Or to their mothers. But they wouldn't notice the difference. You'd be just another hag hiding in a corner. Of course, they might just roast you over the fire and eat you, though you wouldn't be nearly as tasty as that bat."

A blow from her fists knocked each of Kio's arms back to his sides. Then Allukah pulled him inside the Great Hut.

It was a startling structure, as terrifying as it was fascinating, for it stretched a full two hundred feet in diameter with a domed ceiling half that high. The walls were woven from the same rotting brambles as the nine tiers of mud huts scattered around outside it. Each of the tapered columns supporting the roof rested on the body of a young girl who had been kidnapped and dropped into the hole like a chestnut before the heavy posts were rammed down. And some of the wooden columns had sprouted, twining roots around the skeletons of the victims and tapping nourishment from their flesh. The girls were not virgins, of course. Horlas just wouldn't stand still for that kind of waste.

From outside, the sod-blanketed dome of the Great Hut was a mountain overgrown by weeds, briars, and the trunks of small saplings. Young warriors spent their idle hours riding ponies up the side, urging the stumpy animals to carry them all the way to the top while other warriors tried to stop them. Hooves chewed at the eroding walls as climbers met guards, whipping, wrestling, crowding each other so that some fell and were trampled or simply rolled back down to the ground where a ring of sharp stakes waited to impale them. From outside, the Great Hut might have been a colossal garbage heap, or the grave of some long-dead giant.

Inside, Kio squinted through the smoky haze of camel-dung lamps to locate two thrones woven out of gold strips. Workers in the Purjobi mines had dug the glittering metal out of the earth's bowels before shipping the ore to Abbida where it was smelted, refined, and cast into ingots, coins, or candelabras. From there the precious metal headed for the walled city of Centropolis. That was the last time civilized eyes ever saw it. Somewhere along the way, in one of the many canyons carved into the mountains ringing the Sugar Desert, Micar short-circuited the intricate trade routes and bartered blood for gold. Few were strong enough to resist such a bargain. Crowns and scepters were spun into thread for Micar's robes; icons and false teeth were melted down or pounded into strips which later were molded into one of his many thrones.

Crudely cast in unalloyed gold, the soft metal sagged under its own weight. Each of the thrones was studded with emeralds, rubies, tortoise shell, and the fused, colored glass that came out of the ground wherever the ancients once dwelled. On each arm of Micar's throne, lions yawned, their manes flaring into small novas. On the queen's throne were rams, their coiled horns pierced by hooded cobra heads. The eyes of the metal beasts were all plugged by luminous Najucular stones. Suspended directly above the thrones, a gilded propeller slowly revolved, its ground edges slicing through the smoke. If Kio had visited this place a week ago, his sensitive, creative nature would have been repelled by these primitive, awkward attempts at decoration. Now he just turned his head and looked on with dull curiosity as Allukah led him deeper.

The dirt floor of the hut had been compacted by countless feet and dyed an uneven reddish brown by the aral-root wine and blood spilled there over the centuries. Hanging from the poles, shattered headlights reflected lamplight in scanning beacons. There were colored bottles too, twisted and sunken as though melted in a furnace of volcano. But the posts were dominated by the long pelts strung with the dried ears the Horlas claimed in battle. Each one represented the cold ashes of a human life—a man slain, a woman raped, a child ravaged.

Kio's head passed beneath gold cages, empty now except for an occasional skull or odd bone. The doors hung open as though someone had just come along and let the prisoners out for exercise. From the clouds caught in the dark dome, Kio thought he heard chirping, but he could see nothing there.

All along the walls, separated by more straps of dried ears, tapestries were hung. They weren't woven in the camp for no Horla hand had enough dexterity to grip anything smaller than a sword, and that's all they needed to steal some of the most striking images ever bound in thread. There were hunt scenes with graceful riders racing through fields, their mounts trampling over peasants who'd been stupid enough to plant their crops across the hunter's path. Dogs ripped at the throats of does. Streets clogged with traffic. And there were, of course, carnivals of pink flesh where men, women, and occasional beasts of assorted varieties or endowments cavorted, chased one another, caught and sealed themselves together in squirting, squatting, spreading poses. Some figures had their mouths open or stuffed, more had their mouths pressed to or wrapped around. But all were wide eyed and frozen at the instant of eruption, preserved in the suddenness of their guilt, until the slow convected currents on the air sighed, rippling the tapestries into undulating motion. Then once again legs wriggled, pelvises pumped, heads cocked, shuttering. And one of the figures stepped right out of the tapestry.

"Lewylln," Allukah raised her hand, and the coiled whip it clutched so tightly, to call over that figure gliding across the floor.

Dressed in a crimson robe open to just below the waist and bound by a golden girdle, the man must have been eight feet tall. His eyebrows were plucked into thin arches, his lips smeared with a paste to match his robe. A dusting of white powder leant his face a ghostly pallor. His right ear was gone. Above the scar, not a single hair broke the smooth line of his scalp and it was there, in that crystal globe of translucent skin branched into intricate patterns of blue veins, that Kio saw his fate written.

"I have a new toy for you," Allukah thrust Kio forward.

"Oh, Allukah, you only give me your toys after you've broken them." His voice was a flute fluttering toward a higher note. "And oh my, we're a dirty one, aren't we?"

91

One of the long-nailed hands reached out of the billowy sleeves to pull Kio's jaw around. The fingers felt limp, moist, and warm, and they left behind the scent of violets. In the other hand, a short whip pushed out as many tails as a willow tree. Lewylln ran its handle over the contours of Kio's face as though he were molding it.

"But eyes. We do have pretty eyes. And good bones." Slouching with one hand on a hip, he turned to Allukah. "Do you think we can do anything with him, dear? He certainly is *raw* material."

Kio noticed there wasn't even a suggestion of a beard on the man's chin. It was then he realized this wasn't a man at all, but a eunuch.

"He's no good for the cages. There's no fight left in him."

"Well? What do you expect *me* to do with him? I can't work miracles, you know." Lewylln pouted.

"You take him, Lewylln," Allukah took her dagger out of her belt and slid it lightly over her tongue. "And make him like you."

Lewylln's eyes seemed to suck the lamplight right out of the air. Flares swirled around in his sockets while he shuffled forward to gather Kio into the muggy, perfumed folds of his robe.

Chapter 9

Bacchanalia

The sound reached out across the crowded floor of the Great Hut and grabbed him, shaking his skull till it rattled.

Well, maybe they thought it was music. But Kio knew it was noise, without rhythm or harmony. Just noise. More than anything else, the sour racket had the ear-marks of a tinker's wagon hurling down the side of a rocky mountain. The band, if it could be called that, was a rag-tag collection of dented bugles, ox-horn lyres strung with dried intestines, hide drums, and cracked cymbals. Metal clanged as wood snapped and skins vibrated, mixing with the wounded cries of animals and captives, drowning out the gurgle of aral-root wine and the grunting, gymnastic gratifications of the slate-skinned Horlas that were packed inside the hut. From one wall to the next ran a carpet of thrashing, twisted bodies of these gluttonous mongrels. Men grappled with men, with women, or with bears and sheep, squeezing quick pleasure out of coarse, furred flesh before going on to the next.

Kio waded through it all, holding out his wicker basket for dirty fingers to scoop out sweatmeats and pistachio nuts. He poured wine from a silver pitcher into the ragged, topless aluminum cans held under his nose, and took no more than a passing notice of who was lying with whom or with what. After Allukah, after

93

Lewylln, pleasure was just the memory of a tumor that had been ripped out of him. The only body that interested him now was his own. Wretched as it might be, it was the only thing they left him. He didn't know yet that she was following him.

As constant as a shadow, she trailed along behind, always careful so he wouldn't see. Her tiny body, with that translucent skin, was still shrouded in a black cloak, her dark eyes peeking out from the fur hood, and she had to move quickly, bobbing, weaving away from grasping hands or shoving some other body into their clutches instead. She wouldn't let anything stop her. And she wouldn't let him see her—not yet, at least.

The dense, blue smoke of hasket, the locoweed the Horlas puffed into their lungs till they couldn't stand, curled up through the gilded bars above their heads. The cages were filled now, the doors chained shut, and long, needle-tipped lances darted through the bars or floors till they pierced a Teutite prisoner huddled inside, or snapped off against the hide of armadillos or apes. Long-handled pincers grabbed whatever careless finger or tail chanced to stray beyond the bars, cracking knuckles and toes as easily as ice. Often a hot coal bobbed onto a prisoner's belly, or a firebrand into his face. The squeals, and the futile attempts to escape to a far corner where other lances, other pincers lay waiting, incited cheers from grinning Horlas. This was a celebration of their own omnipotence. Here in the hut they had total control over pain. They inflicted it at will, or stopped it, knowing all the while that once they stepped outside these circular walls, they too would be at the mercy of fate. Outside they would shiver and groan, shriek and cry as loud as the next man. Yet inside the hut, for these few hours, they were the masters of these helpless creatures. Watching them squirm, hearing their screams, made the Horlas' own miseries insignificant by comparison. And that made them ecstatic—and twice as thirsty for blood. For these very same reasons, the Horlas weren't particularly delighted about torturing animals. No, animals didn't share the sin of knowing pain could be used as pleasure. Pain was a sensation that never spread outside the skin of the beasts. Instead, it ricocheted around inside their empty eyes, reflecting only the shallows of their real suffering. Their wordless squeals were automatic, without hesitation or shame, and the animals never realized that only luck put them on one side of the bars instead of the other. But animals were stronger than the Teutites. They lived much longer, took a lot more abuse. So once the last squeal was wrung from the last Teutite, the Horlas grudgingly turned to the armadillos and raised their lances toward gorillas and orangutans, resigning themselves to second best.

Kio ignored the screams of the Teutites, though the shrill cries of the animals scraped over his spine. But after a while, even that didn't bother him. It wasn't his pain.

In an unlit alcove facing the backs of the Horlas, stood a statue of the goddess Luka. In front of its hard, naked stone, the sacrificial dung braziers were cold and neglected. Before Allukah came, the Horlas had only the six gods of the plastic loops, their small brains too feeble to imagine the grandeur of unity, or true purpose of one god. But Allukah taught them how to sacrifice to the goddess Luka, how to kneel, how to grovel, and how to plead for favors. The Horlas didn't enjoy kneeling, or giving up their children or slaves to feed the smoldering dung, and most wished they could go back to the original six gods who stayed beneath the mounds with the other garbage and never made nuisances of themselves by asking for sacrifices. However, the Horlas also enjoyed winning battles or living to see the next dawn, and Allukah assured them these things could come only through Luka. So the Horlas obeyed. They sacrificed. They groveled. But there was no battle today. Today the Horlas had everything they wanted, so Luka would have to wait till something went sour.

Mixed in with the men, there were beardless boys with eyelids caked in glitter, lips with paint, and their slim bodies lounged in silk robes that were split along the sides and spread down the middle. Some Horla women stood over them, their waists and breasts bound in studded leather, their hair tied back into tar-coated tails. There were freaks too, with earlobes hanging down to their ankles, four-armed men, or six-legged women. And dwarfs as big as your knee. Pinheads rolled their sore eyes and the two-headed albino squabbled with itself. All of them, Horla and freak, were hand-clasping, mouth-gnawing, nibbling, sucking, eyeless moles burrowing through the soil of bodies, feeling their way, tasting to find out where they were or where they were headed.

And over them, on a platform raised up out of the sea of sweat, sat Micar, Master of the Horlas.

Ringed by the tempered invar of his imperial guards, Micar was an eagle perched above his nest, watching over his featherless fledglings with the most primitive mixture of awe and contempt. Nothing escaped his darting eyes, not a single shudder of pleasure, not a single spasm of pain. These were his subjects, his charges, and he knew them well enough never to relax his vigilance. Even as he hugged Cella, his favorite wife seated on the smaller throne with a jeweled veil shimmering over her face like liquid stars. Even when he fondled her small, pointed breasts and let his prehensile tongue search through the canals of her ear, making her giggle and squirm. Even then Micar kept one eye cocked, scanning over the crowd, marking every scene, every quivering muscle or disappointed curse to see what trouble they portended. Then he'd roar for more wine to be brought in, more hasket, more women, more boys, Teutites—anything to keep the Horlas occupied, buried in their own avalanche of abuse and constantly in motion, exhaustion, or delirium, so the shallow convolutions of their brains didn't get the chance to trap an idea. Micar knew as well as we do that ideas can be bad. After all, hadn't ideas put the world where it was today?

Most of all, Micar watched Amurti, though he knew his young son was spineless without his mother to spur him on.

Kio turned his eyes to Cella who snuggled close to the master, her long legs tucked under her creamy gown. He sneered when she glanced back to the forty other concubines penned away from the men, stewing in the juices of their own jealousy as they returned her glance. And all the while the golden fan spun above the master's head, cutting the haze into thick, cucumber slices that dropped over the royal couple, drying the sweat on Micar's brow and rustling the chestnut ringlets of Cella's hair.

A greedy, wanton creature, Kio thought. But all women were. They let the men go out to be slaughtered, let them masquerade at being warriors or conquerors. And all the while the bitches sat back safe and fattening, pulling the strings, pushing, tempting. Spiders. That's what they were, inviting you in for dinner. It's not long before you find out you're the main course. They're all the same. Every single one of them. With one exception. That woman. The one with the linen cloth who wiped his face. The one with the translucent skin. Where was she? Kio went on, wading through the throng, search-ing, peeking under squirming piles of Horla flesh. He found women and boys wriggling at every probing touch of a Horla. Some even reached out to paw him, slid their greasy hands up under the folds of the blue gown Lewylln had given him. Kio ignored their pinches, their moaning invitations, for he was looking for her, and, anyway, he no longer had what these flesh eaters wanted. Allukah had reconstructed his senses. Lewylln had finished that job.

The eunuch had been ecstatic over the opportunity to permutate Kio's young, if somewhat wilted, body into a miniature parody of his own. Personally he bathed Kio, soaking him in a steaming tub of perfumed water before he ran those soft, soapy hands over the torn muscle, peeling away the scabs, probing, squeezing, inserting those huge fingers into every crevice and hole, nibbling Kio's neck. Once the candidate was dried and powdered, the eunuch unsheathed his razor. With a single stroke, he took from Kio that piece of dangling flesh the Horlas most prize.

The cut was so clean, there wasn't any room for pain. But the shock of what had been done to him took away all his strength. Kio collapsed on the straw-matted floor. He clutched at the wound, writhing as he tried to hold back the flow of blood. It was then Lewylln had thrown him the robe.

"Now you're just like me," Lewylln ran a palm over his own scar, then pouted as Kio, stunned deaf and blind, ignored him.

"No whimpering now. I won't stand for it." Lewylln prodded him with the handle of his many-tailed whip. Kio froze and let the blood flow.

"Oh, he wants sympathy, doesn't he?" Lewylln puckered his lips, kneeling at Kio's side. "You want me to kiss it and make it better, you silly little fool?''

Kio shrank away from the man's hand. No—not a man—a eunuch! Lewylln's face went as red as his robe when he saw the look of aversion. He lashed Kio across his face. Then, back on his feet, Lewylln circled the bath house snorting, sighing, without looking at Kio.

"I've been too easy with you. I thought you'd be different. Allukah always says I'm too soft. Well, I like to be soft. That's the way I am. Do you appreciate that? No. You treat me like the rest of them. It's in your eyes. Don't try to deny it. So maybe I should treat you like I treat the rest of them.''

Lewylln stopped, lashed him again. It wasn't a deep welt like Allukah's bullwhip, but more like a face full of stinging acid.

"I would so like to hear your civilized throat scream, honey. Just to know you're at home. Scream for me, won't you? Show us how they do it back at Centropolis." Lewylln lashed him again.

"The harder I hit, the more you like it. Don't you? You've been praying all your life for something like this to happen to you, haven't you? Well, now's your chance. Come on. Scream for me, love. Scream for m e !' '

Kio never did scream, even though Lewylln was right. Kio did welcome the pain. It made him feel cleaner than the bath. He was paying for it now, paying for everything, for all the years of stupidity he had spent behind the walls of Centropolis, paying for his ego, for the pain he had caused his mother when he was born. Kio was settling his debts, every one of them. The list was long. But when the lashing finally stopped, Kio owed nothing to anybody. And that made him free.

Rolling off a throbbing body, Amurti, Allukah's crag-faced son, clamped Kio's ankle in his hand. His smile was a row of icicles melting over his goatish chin. The red marks of fingernails and teeth etched his shoulders and back. Naked except for his precious copper breastplate and the necklace of enemy teeth rattling against it, Amurti wasn't looking for sweetmeats from the basket slung over Kio's arm. Lifting the hem of the blue robe, he thrust his head underneath it.

"I hear they're crushed your pigeon's eggs," the voice filtered through the blue silk. "Now you'll know that only Horlas are really men."

When that goatish face reappeared, Amurti snatched a fistful of pistachio nuts from the basket and stuffed them into his slobbering mouth. Instead of spitting the shells out, he washed them down with a slug of root wine.

Amurti clenched Kio's ankle as fast as a bear trap, digging dirty nails into the skin. With his other hand he kneaded his own genitals as his glands dumped a new load of hormones into his blood.

"You're a good server, silent and spiritless. I like that. My mother was smart to let you live."

Then he rolled over and swam back into the sea of flesh. Kio passed on. He knew he no longer belonged in the company of men. And all the while his shadow followed, faithfully, silently. Even Amurti wasn't quick enough to grab her.

Outside in the cool air that was laced with the fragrance of fermenting garbage, Kio shuffled through flurries of nipping flies until he stood before the massive oak tub holding the swill that passed for wine. Though the magic aral roots had been strewn over its bottom then covered with Baskla leaves and water according to the traditional recipe, Horlas weren't especially renowned for their patience. Rather than wait the six weeks it would take for the thinnest, weakest true wine to form, they rushed the process by adding vegetable scraps and fruit. Crusts of bread, bones, or an odd Teutite captive were thrown into the bubbling, scummy cauldron. New water was poured in to replace what evaporated or was drained away by thirst, so the vile brew was always changing, never the same, except for the sudden punch of a great fist against your temples, or the sharp pins you felt thrusting into your eyes when you drank it.

When Kio turned the handle of the chrome spigot, a slug of trapped gas sneezed out into his jug. Then a glop of pasty goo, followed by the cloudy maroon wine that coated the silver jug like melted chocolate.

Kio was alone now, unguarded. He might have left the Great Hut and kept on walking. But where would he go? No one was waiting for him, not in Centropolis, not in Somelon. Only the jackals in the hills would be glad to see him, to taste him. Anyway, to escape Kio would have to sneak out through the nine diamond-shaped tiers of Horla ziggurats that were riddled with those nasty, gopher-faced children, those shrewish, turtle-backed women. His body still twitched everytime he thought of those sharp sticks in those dirty little hands. He twisted the spigot closed and turned back to the hut. It was then she caught his eye.

He'd seen the image before, when an autumn moon reflected off the rolling gray surface of the Tent River, or in the quarry when he looked down a deep shaft and saw a glowing Najucular stone at the very bottom. But when the image met his eye this time, it blinked out suddenly as the woman hid her translucent face in her hood.

Kio dropped the jug to chase his own shadow into the hut. But as soon as he ran through the door, the noise and smoke, the light attacked his face like the lashes from Lewylln's whip. By the time he recovered, she was gone again, lost somewhere in the crowd. Kio turned back to fetch his silver jug. And when he passed out through the doorway, his shadow precipitated out of the darkness to follow him.

Despite the commotion rumbling through the hut, the atmosphere was relatively calm, at least if you compared it to what happened during the feast. Micar, as was his right, had been served first. The seared carcass of an ostrich, its long neck dragging over the floor with head still attached, had been split open at the foot of the throne. Then Micar, slowly and deliberately, had taken out his amber dagger and sliced away the tenderest morsels for himself and his bride while the rest of the drooling Horlas looked on, struggling with various degrees of failure, to keep their muscles under control.

Micar ate as fast as he could, swallowing chunks whole, for he wanted to end the ritual quickly. He knew his mongrel warriors were in the throes of covetous agony. They couldn't hold out for more than a few minutes. But Cella took full, excruciating advantage of her position and nibbled on a wing bone, kissing the tips of her small fingers, lingering over the tiniest scrap of meat before flinging the bone into the crowd.

When the Horlas pounced on that bone, fighting one another for the prize, she clapped her greasy hands together in glee. Then she asked Micar, with a pout, for another piece. He gave it to her because he loved her and couldn't bear to disappoint her, despite his misgivings. And it wasn't until she tired of taunting the crowd that the royal meal reached its conclusion. With a sigh of relief, Micar called for the Teutite oxen to be brought in. At the sight of the roasted, unbutchered beef, the Horlas went mad.

In a single blink of Kio's eye, seventeen carcasses were stripped of skin and meat. Then, in a merciless wave of grinding, the skeletons disappeared. Cages of white doves and long-necked swans were dragged in and smashed open. The doves were quick, so most of them escaped by flying high into the rafters where they hoped to be safe. The swans, however, were too slow. They were ripped apart, stuffed into bloody mouths while they were still white, raw, and fluttering.

But the appetite of these savages continued to rage. They lit bonfires on the floor of the hut, led in camels, sheep, giant kimodo lizards. Fur, hide, and scales smoldered as they were held down, live and kicking, over the flames, sending up clouds of acrid smoke along with their screams. Yet the Horlas couldn't wait for the fires. Before the life was roasted out of the beasts, their talons reached out and tore. Smoky meat slid into bottomless gullets. Still-twitching heads were tossed through the air or kicked like Baba balls. The mushy brains were scooped into bearded mouths, eyeballs swallowed like plums. And still the gluttonous orgy reigned unchecked. That's when the Teutite captives were thrown onto the fires. The Horlas didn't care much for that meat. It was much too sweet. But once they ate it, those who didn't throw it back up were no longer hungry.

Kio watched it all with the disgust only a once-civilized man could know, though his lip curled back a bit less each time he sneered. Refilling his basket, he passed back into the crowd, pausing only briefly over the one-eyed twins, Mishla and Cular. Kio let his eyes roam, hoping they'd settle on his shadow again, so he never saw the way the two warriors were occupying themselves with another set of twins—a young pair of hermaphrodites dressed and painted half as women, half as men, as though they were two phases of the moon, as though one man and one woman had been split down the middle and joined to their opposites. To Mishla and Cular, this was the best of both worlds. They worked over these dual natures with spitting fury. Between bouts, the archers sent their feathered shafts into the air and the smoky clouds rained down the bodies of white doves.

In another round corner of the hut Careem, his stump bared and twitching like the head of a seal, toyed with his own special pet. It was a black Watut without arms or legs who squirmed along the dirt floor like a grub.

Kio ducked beneath the garlands strung into tents and he kept his eyes averted from the crosses hanging upside down on the wooden columns, for the figure tacked on those brass and wood strips would only remind him of that ache in his shoulders again. And he didn't need that. As a whole, he was doing fine, adapting to it all. And as the stench of burned flesh temporarily gave way to frankincense and hasket, Kio congratulated himself for surviving, for not letting anything bother him, for forgetting. Then Allukah came in and it all came rushing back.

She stood blocking the doorway, scanning those cloudy yellow eyes through the haze. When he saw her, Kio remembered every sickening detail of the past week and he stopped chasing his shadow.

Chapter 10

Queen of the Horlas

She stood there, her massive body dwarfed by the tremendous bronze doors of the Great Hut, while bones and crushed drinking cups whistled past her head. With each whole minute that went by without anyone noticing her, those clouded eyes bloomed into yellower moons as bright as the yolks of shattered Roc's eggs, swelling, ready to burst. In the smoky patterns drifting inside those two globes, he could read his fate.

Once again, Allukah had done the impossible deed, a feat equal to, if not exceeding, the day she faced the full fury of the Centropolis guards alone. Two thousand strong, she had turned them single-handedly, with no weapon save the arm of the guard commander which she tore from his socket and wielded as a club. This time, however, it was not a test of courage on the battle-field or a triumph of wits in outflanking the enemy. No, this time Allukah had concentrated all her strength in squeezing—not a camel through the eye of a needle, which would have been child's play by comparison. Rather, Allukah had shoehorned her bulging flesh into the silver armor looted from the caravan, the silver armor Kio had carried here on his back. From every crevice above, below and behind the metal plates, fat leaked out like dough through a baker's fingers. The leather straps creaked loud and dry under the terrible strain of her breathing. On the chestplate, the ruby eyes tipping the breasts bulged, about to pop out, while the silver mouth was contorted into a groan. The hawk's-head helmet sat cocked on her scalp as if it had been flying casually by when it chanced to crash into that tangle of greasy hair and died of shame.

Trying with diminishing success to keep herself cool and roughly composed, she popped another Najucular stone into her mouth. The hair on her lip curled into a mustache as she swallowed.

From Allukah's left hand, a leash ran to a spiked collar ringing the throat of a girl crouched on all fours. Nude, except for an emerald belt around her tapered waist, the pet's hair had been harshly bleached, as had her skin till it was a wild, blotchy coat of spots. The girl panted, her breasts hanging down in small, quivering funnels.

And still the Horlas, spry as puppies, played on the floor of the Great Hut, yelping and biting and paying no notice. Allukah stretched so hard to make herself taller that a buckle snapped on the back of the armor. More fat leaked out. Allukah steamed.

The pet, sensing her master's impatience, tugged at the leash, snapping at passing buttocks, and earned herself a cuff on the ear when Allukah roughly yanked her back to heel.

More minutes whistled past. Allukah spied Micar, then Cella on the throne to his right. That was an insult she couldn't handle; or at least it provided the excuse she needed. Her arm shot out. She grabbed the nearest handful of Horla and hurled the failing body forty feet over the heads of the crowd to strike Amurti square in the copper breastplate. Another buckle snapped off her armor.

Instantly alert, Amurti pulled his dagger out of the body that had knocked him to the ground and untangled himself from the limp arms and legs of the corpse. Holding his dripping blade out in front of him, ready for the next attack, his searching gaze fell on his mother standing there waiting, smoldering. So Amurti dove back into the pile of bodies to resurface with a unicorn bugle pressed to his lips.

The horn released a sound identical to a bubble of sulfurous gas bursting out of a volcano filled with molten lava—the belch of the earth. The raw volume of the fanfare was enough to freeze all the pumping bodies, all the chewing mouths, in the hut. And Allukah gave every eye just enough time to find her before she began her march toward the throne. That's when the third strap on her armor let go.

Kio, caught in the crowd, winced as the Horla queen came closer, anticipating the next outrage she would work on his battered body. But she strutted on by him without a word, without even a snort. She might have overlooked him. He was just a small face in a great crowd, though Kio knew nothing escaped those opaque eyes of hers. No. She was through with him, just as the female wasp lays her eggs in one carcass before moving on to the next.

Allukah leaped onto the throne platform and hovered over Cella like an angry cumulonimbus, covering the tiny queen with her shadow. Cella flinched, grabbing for Micar's arm. With his strength in her fingers, she had the nerve to return Allukah's stare.

"Why is this slut in my throne?" Allukah wrapped her huge paw around the golden arm of the chair, completely covering the ram's head decorating it.

"It's not yours, you cow," Cella hissed, scratching Allukah's hand so hard her long, painted nails cracked.

Allukah smiled down at her.

"Those are my thrones," Micar snapped. "I choose who sits with me and who does not."

"And tonight you choose me." With one hand, Allukah scooped Cella up by the ankles, with the other she slapped her like midwife slaps a newborn child. And like that child, Cella let out a wail that wasn't muffled till Allukah tossed her behind the throne to rejoin her sisters, the rest of the concubines. That's when the fourth strap snapped and her armor began to sag.

Micar stiffened, wrapping his hands tightly around the lions' manes till the knuckles turned white. He would have liked to kill her right there where she stood, just to show them all who was king. But he knew that show would cost him more than a few large chunks of his own hide. Allukah's death would extract an extravagant toll, and right at that moment it didn't seem at all to be a shrewd bargain. So in his wisdom, the master of the Horlas decided to bide his time until he had a better advantage.

Micar felt the hot eyes of Cella burning through his back. Though he truly loved her, he did nothing.

"Food!" Allukah bellowed, dropping her weight into the throne so the golden legs buckled under the strain. Her pet sprawled panting at her feet.

Scurrying out of the crowd came Amurti, his tooth necklace inlaid into the soft metal of his breastplate by the force of the body she'd thrown at him. In his hands was a bowl of steaming meat. Allukah patted her faithful son on his flat head, then dug her paw into the grease. The pet purred, nuzzling against Amurti's legs.

"A good boy," Allukah leaned into Micar's ear. "He'll make the Horlas a fine leader one day."

A fistful of meat smothered the words. Her teeth bared to rip at the bones, but as soon as the taste coated her sandpaper tongue, the lips warped into a meat-spitting scream.

"You fool!" Allukah buried her foot in Amurti's chest, crumpling the copper breastplate. The son reeled. The bowl sailed into the crowd. Taking this for a sign that all was right again, the Horlas scrambled, fighting over the bones. The pet sank its teeth in Amurti's calf.

"How dare you serve me the flesh of some weed-eating doe! This body cries out for red meat—red, dripping meat ripped from a beast that eats other beasts, from a beast that has already taken the best parts of the kill and thrown the rest to jackals!"

Scrambling to his feet, Amurti ran wild eyes around the hut. The rest of the meat had disappeared long ago, so not even scrap of fur, or a tooth was left. The Teutites were gone, so were the swans. Then those eyes settled on Kio, brightening with an idea.

Amurti took a step forward, tripping over the limbless torso of Careem's grubby Watut pet. The royal son grabbed it instead and limped off for fire. Amurti's mother would have meat, the meat of a carnivor.

Careem pulled out his five-foot scimitar. He wasn't ready to fight with Amurti over the Watut. But someone in the crowd was about to lose all his limbs and take the pet's place on the floor.

Kio turned back into the sea of Horlas, his basket swinging from side to side, buffeted by wave after wave of snatching hands. That might have been his body Amurti threw on the fire. It would have been the final insult to be torn apart and cracked by those stalactite teeth of Allukah, to slide over her rasping tongue, to splash into the fermenting cauldron of that enormous belly. Then the supreme irony, to be absorbed into her blood and become a living part of her flesh. Though his nerves were numb, his cheeks tingled, especially where Lewylln's dull razor had scraped off his beard. It was the flesh of relief spreading out from his brain.

At that point, Kio wouldn't have admitted it, and it's certain that nobody would have cared to ask him, but somewhere deep in the darkest recesses of his psyche he began to tolerate these creatures. The next step after that would be respect. Yet how could anyone ever respect these insects? Well, it wasn't the kind of respect you'd feel for your mother, or for any human, in fact. Better, think of a rattlesnake, its argyle scales iridescent in the sun as it slithers toward your leg, coming to rest with its head on your foot. Instantly you respect those fangs folded back and hidden out of sight somewhere in that tongue-flickering mouth. You'd give all you had to the serpent, surrender the feeblest right, if only he'd turn those acquisitive eyes to some other prey and let you go on breathing.

It was that way with the Horlas. They'd taken everything Kio had and for the first time in his life he realized that possessions and rights were as illusory, as ephemeral as the hasket smoke curling out of the Horlas' lungs. After all, what kind of perverted creature hides behind forty-foot stone walls to scratch away at granite with steel chisels like some frustrated tom cat sharpening his claws for a mouse that never comes? That wasn't the way a man spends his life. Amurti knew that instinctively. Kio saw the answer in his eyes when the warrior picked the limbless Watut off the ground. Amurti wanted a man to feed his mother—red muscle drenched with hormones. They all knew it. Kio wasn't a man anymore.

The screams came louder, more piercing, rolling across the hut to strike him solidly in the head. Kio shook them off, and those that followed. Only when he tipped his silver pitcher and found it dry did he let himself look in the direction of those latest screams.

Then he saw broken Horla bodies flying into the air, tumbling, before disappearing under the feet of the scattering crowd.

Driving them on came Maskim astride his rearing, bucking mule. Like war paint, the fresh welts from Allukah's whip cut through the hairs on his face. The cretin swung a thick length of knotted robe, weighted with stone, that had been dipped in tar and rolled in broken green glass. So the crowd parted before Maskim just as clods of dirt are thrown out by the blade of a plow. From one end of the hut to the next, he cut a wide furrow, then turned around to start another. Foaming warriors leaped at him, tore at the reins, but Maskim beat everyone of them down with his rope or his snorting mule trampled them with silver-shod hooves.

"Clear out of the way, you vomiting buzzards. Make way for the dancers!" The cretin yelled, plowing on. He wore a cloak of shredded green plastic and hot sweat basted his gnarled body as though it were a capon.

On the throne, Allukah clapped her fat hands together, happy to see the cretin.

"He's the only one that can make me laugh," she bellowed to no one in particular. Another strap on the armor gave way. The breastplate dangled from her shoulders.

Kio made his way to the far wall where he'd be out of Maskim's range. From there he watched the clearing of the floor. The only thing that surprised him about the whole affair was how Maskim managed to get back out of the hut without anybody eating his mule.

When the cretin reappeared, a plastic toilet seat was slung over the mule's neck. From that plump, white horseshoe, a harness of braided thongs dragged a flat platform into the hut. Once Kio saw the bright veils of the dancers riding that platform, he turned away to refill his basket. He didn't have any interest in those kind of things anymore.

In all, five dancers tottered stiff as figurines till they reached the center of the freshly cleared floor. Then they flung themselves off the sliding platform and began to dance. One dancer was draped in red, the others in green, blue, gold, and black sprays of gauzy silk that sweetly kissed the rolling contours of their bodies as they ran and billowed out into the flower petals when they twirled. The folds floated up to offer a quick glimpse of white or brown, the pink undulating nakedness broken only by matching jewels held like sparkling monocles in their navels. Then the colored curtains dropped down again, blocking the view so quickly that the eye scarcely believed what it had seen. In a warped marriage of modesty and the carnal, each dancer was veiled so only wild eyes peeked out of their faces.

The Horlas went crazy. Whooping and slapping, they surged inward threatening to crush the frail dancers just as bears roll over buttercups in the meadows. But Micar's imperial guards were there, their whips licking at the scarred faces of the Horlas till they retreated. The dancers swirled on, sweeping over the floor toward the thrones. The Horlas went into tantrums, stomping their feet, grabbing themselves in frustration.

With the ignition of these five colorful flames, the atmosphere inside the Great Hut crystallized. Under the agitation of their dizzying reels, what had, only a second before, been a sty clogged with wallowing swine, became a temple of reverent worshippers. The crude band strained its chords, refining the din till it bordered on music, doing a weak justice to the flicking toes of the dancers. The Horla men spit in their callused palms, smoothed back their tangled hair as they stretched out trying to straighten their knotted backbones to appear

112

taller. Their women, fully jealous, covered their own nakedness, scraped the dirt from under their cracked fingernails with their teeth, and washed out their mouths with aral-root wine. Taking sticks of charcoal from the fires, they darkened their eyebrows, and burnished their cheeks with red dust from the floor (as though there were ever a Horla woman innocent enough to blush). Of course these hags were aware that, even in the dim eyes of their men, they couldn't come within a light year of the luscious dancers. Yet the Horla women could count, at least to five. In the Great Hut there were over six thousand sex-crazed Horlas. These women were preparing themselves for the overflow. They'd get their chance when the dancers were done stirring up the men, if only by default.

As quick as a gust of the west wind, the rancid odor of sweat and grease blew away. The choking smoke rising from the cookpits took on a fresh fragrance as fistfuls of incense were cast into the coals. The metallic litter of the band now assumed a smooth, moody light enough to let the tinkle of the dancers' finger cymbals trickle through. Even the cackling harem went suddenly quiet and still until the Great Hut held an image in its eye that was indistinguishable from the bazaar of some exotic, yet civilized city like Centropolis.

Mostly, it was an illusion, a sneaky trick of the mind and senses the dancers were skilled at performing. They were artists, trained from birth and trusted with the secrets of muscular kinetics. Whether gyrating across the center of the floor, or skirting the rim of the crowd, they retained complete control. Their eyes knew precisely when to flash, their legs when to skip, their stomachs when to wiggle and churn. But most important of all, they'd learned when to run before a greedy hand could grab them.

Four of the dancers had dark hair with skin the color of the sassafalous roots that poked out of the banks on the side of the road. They were dressed in red, blue, gold, and black. The fifth dancer was taller than the rest, her body long and tapered, and her veils green as the summer grass, her hair a golden dandelion above a sea of black weeds. Her arms were white swans sliding out from under the sleeves, swimming through the air, wriggling and wrapping around her body. Her tiny feet patted so lightly over the earthen floor that not even a puff of dust rose up as high as those ankles circled by strings of yellowed bone. Each time those high-stepping feet kicked out, the bones rattled ever so softly.

Cella was nudged out of Micar's mind now. By his side on the throne, even Allukah lost her foul breath at the sight of the golden girl. Grabbing the arms of the throne, the queen of the Horlas pulled her weight forward with enough force to snap the necks of the metal rams, and under her voice she took a vow to the neglected goddess Luka to forsake the bodies of mere men from that day on just for a taste of the snug body of this single dancer. Allukah was caught by an hypnotic snare, attracted like darkness to light, chaos to order, male to female.

All eyes were drawn by the jade top spinning round the floor. Her hair flared out into a wheel of fire. Her skirt sliced through the air in many green blades threatening to lop off the hand of anyone who dared to touch her. And when the gauzy folds whirled up above her thighs, above the small patch of corn silk moist with sweat, they revealed her navel stuffed with a glittering emerald. Spinning faster, the wind-rippled snow of her ribs appeared.

The four other dancers tried to ignore the showoff, though they couldn't help noticing the way the attention of the crowd deserted them for the woman in green. Aroused by the slight, their envy festered till a competition spontaneously erupted between them. Each took her turn trying to outdo the green dancer while the remaining three urged her on, conserving their strength for their chance. When that chance came, red, blue, gold, then black vaulted and glided, cartwheeled and spun faster than dustdevils. Sometimes they hurled themselves into the crowd, pulling their gowns open and shoving their musky genitals or breasts into the faces of panting men, then pulling away an instant before they would have been caught. But more times than not, the hand fast enough to touch them pushed them out of the way for blocking the view of the green whirlwind moving across the floor as if she were alone.

The four dancers shrieked like wounded cats, ripped away their veils to spit at the golden-haired girl. They kicked and throttled the crowd as their frustration made them careless and then a hand would reach out to pluck a dancer off the floor. One by one they disappeared with only a strangled cry and a pile of Horla bodies to show they had ever danced in the Great Hut. Then only the golden-haired girl was left.

She danced. It was a dance no living man, woman, or Horla had ever seen before. The music became a swarm of bees, pursuing her, always a beat behind those swimming hands, out of step with those flashing feet, the looping thrust of her hips. Imperceptibly her circles widened as this apparition drifted toward the thrones. In charge of every muscle, she dipped and glided, leaning backward till her head touched the ground and her four limbs formed the legs of a shivering table that was her torso. Then a flick of her feet wheeled hips over head and she was standing again. But she wouldn't pause till she arrested every pair of eyes in the hut—

115

every pair except Kio's.

Faster. Her feet prancing, her fingers dragonflies sewing the mouths of the Horlas shut, binding their senses so tight they were helpless manikins. Faster. Faster she spun, till their dizzy heads bobbed and their bodies staggered. Faster, till she twirled round before the thrones, leaped high into the air to come down hard, her feet digging into the earth.

The music died. The only movement came from the gentle heaving of her chest. The only sound, the soft cooing of the white doves hiding in the rafters somewhere above her head.

Allukah was the first to break the trance. Shot with a need for this body she was born to possess, the queen of the Horlas lunged, clawing away the green gauze covering the dancer's pulsating chest. For a single beat of the heart, that colossal body of hers was paralyzed by the sight of the white mounds falling, rising, stretching with each breath, lying just inches from her nose. Sweat poured out of Allukah's forehead, washing a green tint into her foggy eyes, then the last strap snapped off her armor. The breastplate fell. Allukah pounced, frenzily taking one of those breasts all the way into her mouth while she cradled the other in her paw. With the hawk's head helmet still dangling on her head, it looked like the bird was straining with all its might to lay a great white egg on the dancer's chest.

But now Micar stirred. At his signal, the twins abandoned their hermaphrodites and latched onto the dancer's arms. Mishla pulled hard on the left. Cular on the right, pinning the golden girl where she stood.

Allukah went on slobbering, never noticing the royal sons. She was as close to heaven as she would ever be. Then pain exploded in her head when Micar stepped up to plant the full force of his steel toe at the base of Allukah's spine.

The breast coughed out of her mouth. With a piercing squeal, the queen of the Horlas rolled off, bouncing across the floor till the hawk's head helmet fell away, its neck broken.

Now Amurti came flying out of the crowd, his eyes bubbling with hate and wine as he hurled toward his father. But Careem inserted himself between the two and the sight of his naked stump was enough to make Amurti stop. The son didn't even wait for the five-foot scimitar to leap from its sheath. Instead, he turned to his mother who lay on her face with that queen-sized rump jutting up into the air. He tended to her wounds.

The way cleared, Micar moved closer to the jade beauty. Cular and Mishla twisted their grips, tilting the dancer back so the master of the Horlas could step between her outstretched legs. Micar tore the skirt away, leaving her naked except for the veil. The eye of Cular, the eye of Maskim bulged, rolling at the sight, and planning their turns that would come when the master was finished.

Micar's stiff fingers took a few minutes to find the knot of the girdle hidden beneath his overhanging belly, then a few more were lost before he could unravel it. The britches fell to his knees. He looked deep into the dancer's eyes, savoring the emotion shimmering inside them when she saw what kind of man was Micar, Master of the Horlas. When she saw the fourteen inches of him that had sired so many sons.

Now the twins bent her body further back and with a burp, Micar grabbed her legs, smiling when he felt the way the skin of her thighs shivered like blankets over the heads of terrified children. Micar lifted her lips, brushed aside that small tuft of corn silk protecting the pink lips, and reared back for the thrust.

A tiny foot stirred, flicking off the floor at the precise moment Micar lunged. Propelled by those same powerful thigh muscles, the foot met him at top speed and drove those fourteen inches of solid Horla flesh all the way back inside of Micar's body.

Micar's eyes spun around in their sockets till all you could see were the whites. His wet mouth dropped open and he tottered there for a long second. Then he fell flat on his face, without bouncing, without rolling.

It took no more than a twitch of her arms to send the twins crashing into each other over her head. Then, standing on the throne platform above them all, it was her hand that reached up to rip away the last stitch of her clothes—the veil.

"Sheryl!" Allukah screamed, clutching her buttocks as she squirmed in Amurti's embrace.

"Sheryl!" the hord of Horlas roared with one voice and suddenly there was a tremendous pressure pushing at the walls.

The Somelon's body shone brilliantly as the moon, though once she spied her mother's armor lying on the ground in front of that fat sausage Allukah, a crimson luminescence spread over Sheryl's skin. It was anger. And not just any anger. It was Somelon anger, the rage that lit up a world lost in the darkness. Sheryl took the first step toward the queen of the Horlas.

The Horlas stampeded in panic. Even though they outnumbered her six thousand to one, even though the crush of their bodies alone should have been enough to destroy her, they scattered. The Horlas had fought this white witch before and she'd taught them how much real virtue there can be in cowardice.

"Sheryl!" Careem threw his one-armed body in her path. Beneath his dark, swirling eyes, the tips of his mustache wagged like the bushy tails of two squirrels. All his lonely, desperate prayers had been answered now that he had the green-eyed Somelon in front of him, naked and unarmed. His five-foot scimitar was already in the air above his head when the catcher's mask clamped down to protect his face. The empty stump that had been his arm before he met Sheryl on the battlefield vibrated, wild as a bird about to fly. Then the sword came slicing through the air.

Sheryl leaped, the blade whistling just under her feet. Landing on the throne, she reached up to tear the sweeping gold propeller from its mount. Careem's scimitar took another cut at her. Parrying it with one of the golden blades, she spun the propeller around to meet the next thrust of the sword, slicing Careem's arm off cleanly at the elbow. Both the arm and the scimitar clutched in its hand flew on past the throne and pierced the frantic chest of Cella, impaling her to the hut's wall.

Holding together what was left of his groin, Micar struggled to his feet in time to see his favorite wife hanging there like a glove on a tack, though he wasn't given any time to mourn her. The golden propeller spun again, chopping through his neck. The severed head bounced into the crowd and the Horlas fled the blood-spurting ball as if it were chasing them, as if they thought that bearded mouth could still bite or call out the name of the woman who had lopped it off.

"Sheryl!"

In the packed hut, the word spread like range fire. Horlas trampled each other, tearing, their swords slicing down any that stood in their way, just as machetes cut through jungle vines. They crammed the exits, blocking the way with their bodies. Others attacked the walls, pounding new exits through the sticks and dried mud as they rushed to escape the death being sown by the hands of the woman they believed could not be killed. To a Horla, being slain by a woman meant you'd come back as a woman in the next life. And you wouldn't come back as a woman like Sheryl. There was no woman like Sheryl.

Sheryl turned to pounce on Allukah, but the spot where Amurti had tended his aching mother was now deserted. Leaping back onto the throne, the Somelon swept those keen, green eyes over the hut. It was no use. The Horla bitch was gone. She'd escaped Sheryl's vengeance again, and with her went the treasured armor, the silver breastplate and hawk's head helmet.

It was cold rage the drove her on after that, pure and blind. Vaulting off the throne platform, she spun the golden propeller and fed the blades into the backs of the Horlas who were still trying to flee. Chunks of bloody flesh clogged the air as the Somelon cut her way through to the far wall, then changed direction and began cutting toward the other. Yet nowhere in that shredded pile of arms, legs, and heads, did she find a trace of Amurti, nor a sign of which way Allukah had gone.

Then the Great Hut was still. Sheryl stood atop the mound of corpses, surveying the gift of death she had brought to the Horlas. From their dark perches in the rafters, white doves soared down to rest on her bare shoulders, cooing their gratitude into her ears. The wind came whistling in through the holes torn in the walls of the hut, carrying with it the red-necked vultures whose feast was about to begin. Only Horla blood covered her body and it already began to crust. When she twisted around, it cracked like mud drying in the sun.

Sheryl's eyes scanned over the gilded cages, poked around columns, and skimmed across the delicately woven tapestries until they settled on a swatch of blue cloth resting in a far corner. Then Sheryl slid off the pile of bodies and shyly walked in that direction.

She found him huddled there, clutching the broken hand of a Horla woman who'd been trampled in the stampede. From the marks on the dirt floor, Sheryl could tell he'd dug her out from the piles and dragged her aside.

"Kio," she whispered his name so softly he didn't seem to hear. "I've come to take you home."

His lids fluttered as his eyes left the corpse and found Sheryl standing there. They flickered for a moment, as though he were trying to remember something, before a gust of dusty wind blew the flame out and they were vacant again. Kio's chin sagged back to his chest, the eyes to the crushed body in his hands.

"Kio! It's me. Sheryl. I've slain the Horlas. You're free again." Then, with an eager smile playing on her lips, she added, "Won't you wash their blood from my body with your hands?"

"Why don't you kill me too? Like you killed her?"

Baring his teeth, Kio shouted without opening his mouth. As though afraid to hear more of this, the doves tilted their wings into the wind and were gone.

"Kio, what's wrong? You're my man and I'm—"

"I am a man no longer. I'm no good to you now. Leave me here to die with the rest of them."

Then he started to cry. They weren't sobs of relief, of fear, nor pain. He cried only because he was still alive and the small, stiff hand laying so cold in his own, that hand that had wiped the dirt and blood from his face when first Kio entered this devil's camp, that hand would never move again.

Sheryl stood over him as he sobbed, helpless as no Somelon should ever be. The muscles of her body sagged slightly as the wind chilled them. Then she knelt, took the small man's body into her arms and lifted him as gently as she knew how.

"Leave me alone. Go away. I'm no good to you anymore. I'm no good to anyone."

Sheryl twisted Kio around so the lifeless hand pulled out of his grip. He hit at her, pounding his fists into her face. She never flinched. And when his weak fury was exhausted and Kio started sobbing again, Sheryl carried him out of the hut and into the night.

Chapter 11

Trickster

"Where's Allukah?"

The voice called out again, but it was distant, skirting only the farthest fringes of his awareness, so he paid it no mind. Kio lay propped in the hollow of an aral tree, right where she'd placed him, his face speckled by the few rays of sunlight that leaked through the knotted branches ragged with leaves. That weak, shifting light couldn't begin to compete with the volcano smoldering just a few yards away. The Great Hut had burned all night, driving away the darkness as completely as a comet dropped out of the sky, and the nine diamond-shaped tiers of small Horla huts were fireflies drawn to the flame after Sheryl put a torch to everyone of them.

Somewhere inside that inferno was the tiny body of the woman who so tenderly sponged the suffering out of Kio's face. For her trouble she'd been trampled, her glowing, translucent skin pounded purple and black, her fragile bones splintered. By now the heat would have boiled the juices out of her and baked the flesh into ashes that flaked away to be swept into the sky by blazing currents.

In a flurry of black snow, these ashes returned to earth, settling on Kio's cheeks. They carried back the dirt she had wiped away and they canceled that one small act of pity now that it was so obvious who had lured this death to her. It was Kio's fault.

He knew it the instant he found her lying there with her pale skin empty as a lamp after the wick had been blown out. Sheryl had snuffed it out, trampled over still another innocent life. And the real crime was that the Somelon did it without a twinge of hate or malice. She did it without knowing, without caring one way or the other. It was just another cricket smashed under the racing wheels of a Somelon's chariot, and only one person in the universe knew how precious a thing had been lost. Kio knew. And that secret, along with everything else, was just too much for his scarred shoulders to bear.

"Where's Allukah?" Sheryl's lips shaped the question with precisely the same monotone she used the first time she asked it. Without bothering to look at the prisoner, she gave the chain in her hand a sharp tug that snapped his head back. He gagged.

Since Allukah dragged him to this camp, Kio had known only one other person. Lewylln had treated him in the same way a groom cares for other people's pets: clipping their nails, washing their coats, or bobbing their wagging tails. The eunuch was never really cruel if you took into account how low on the totem pole a dog or a cat usually rates. Finishing the job started by the tiny, translucent woman, Lewylln had bathed and perfumed Kio's body with aggressive, curious hands. Sure he'd been rough at times, uncompromising, and he'd cut Kio like they cut away your foreskin when you enter certain tribes, even if Lewylln did take something more than a foreskin. There were the whippings which made Kio feel cleaner than the baths, and the smooth blue silk gown sliding over the welts of his back gave him back some of that pride he'd lost between here and Centropolis. Then Kio stopped being a pet and became a novice, a trainee. Lewylln would have taught him how to act, how to function in a new life with as little friction as possible.

Once he'd learned the rules, rewards could be won and, in the same way, punishments avoided. Maybe it wasn't the kind of life he was used to, but it had its own kind of security and Kio grasped at it when it was offered. Lewylln wasn't a saint. Not by any stretch of the imagination. He wasn't a demon either. He was only a man—well, half a man—who was charting a course somewhere down the middle, tacking from side to side through a heavy wind, and Kio could have gone along for the ride. But then Sheryl had come here and Kio could feel the leash tightening around his neck again. She wanted to take him back. He'd be her pet. And when Sheryl learned what the hairless giant had been doing with her pet, she went berserk.

Probably Lewylln deserved to die. Who knows what kind of wickedness he had to work to secure his rank in the Horla hierarchy? But Kio knew little of that. He could only imagine, so he took no pleasure in Sheryl's vengeance. She forced him to watch as she staked the giant's perfumed and powdered body over the still-smoldering ashes of one of the huts. It was morning then, so early the sun hadn't lifted itself over the horizon. Yet there was plenty of light to see that those painted lips didn't wince, not even when the hidden embers burned through the red robe and melted into the ivory skin of his back. Kio admired Lewylln then, and hoped the ordeal would end there, quickly and honorably. But Sheryl whistled and the hyenas came trotting out from cover.

The sneering, yellow-black beasts formed a chattering circle around the prisoner. Though one of them dared to bare its teeth to Kio, maybe thinking he was one of the prizes, a swift kick from a Somelon foot sent the mangy body hurling back into the pack to lick its wounds.

She started with Lewylln's toes, inscribing a fine line

around the first joint with a dagger, then snapping the bone with a pop, as you might do to the claw of a boiled crab. Turning it over slowly in her fingers, she examined the bloody digit closely as if she were expecting it to beg for its life, before she tossed it into the air. It landed in the mouth of the hyena with the longest neck.

Sheryl waited for some sign from Lewylln—a groan, a curse. When it didn't come, she brushed the golden hair away from her face and bent over the next toe.

One by one, the brightly polished toes disappeared down the gullets of the grinning animals. It took a long time for Sheryl was careful to let the pain subside between cuts, and she made sure that Lewylln stayed conscious to watch his pampered body consumed by a pack of snarling hyenas. Fingers, feet, arms and legs went the same way. Through it all, Lewylln stayed silent, and the only sign of pain showed in the way he kept rolling his blue eyes toward Kio. But Kio had shut his own eyes to all of this at the beginning.

The screaming didn't start until Sheryl placed her palm under Lewylln's bald head to lift it high enough off the ground for him to see that only the torso was left. Then the knife made a neat circular incision down where Lewylln's chubby buttocks had once been. The very tip of his intestines was offered to a pair of drooling jaws. When those teeth snapped shut and the animal ran, Lewylln was turned inside out.

Maybe Lewylln did deserve to die. But no one deserved to die that way, with the possible exception of the mind that conceived such an atrocity.

"Where is Allukah?"

The chain from Sheryl's hand hung loosely up to the crossbar of the village gate where it ran through the looped tail of one of the brass monkeys. From there it dropped straight down to the place where Maskim's neck should have been, were he a normal man, and only that bubbly head kept the metal noose from slipping off. Maskim had no chin. His plastic shirt was ripped down to his waist like a peeled green banana, exposing a chest so lumpy the bones of his skeleton might simply have been dumped into a blotched skin bag to fill the space between his shoulders. Except for his face where the hair grew thickest, isolated tufts of coarse stubble poked out all over him as the weeds poked out of the desert sand. Wounds from Allukah's whip were still fresh on the cretin's hide and his arms were tied to his side so each time the chain jerked tight, it pulled him up on his toes. Silhouetted against the sky, he twisted like a caterpillar squirming on a strand of sparkling silk.

Sprawled across a suede couch, her green robe open to the air, Sheryl tugged at the chain. The links sprang tight. Maskim squealed.

Was this the same woman Kio had sworn to love? What kind of creature spewed such merciless vengeance? How dark, how utterly bottomless a mind could conceive such tortures, then have the uninhibited savagery to carry them out? Was this what it meant to be a Somelon? If so, what did that make him for having been seduced by her, for surrendering to her? Sure, he'd been a man then, as flawed, as foolish as the next. And everybody knows that men are mean, petty little creatures.

That's why they so cherished women who were pure and isolated from the taint of men, who like precious flowers, were sealed away in the shade where they wouldn't wilt and were only taken out on special occasions to be worshipped. Prostrate before such an intricate, wonderful image, a man could believe there was more to life than spit, sweat, blood and dying. Overwhelmed by reverence in the presence of a goddess, a man was afraid to speak lest he break the spell. And when the rude nose of the world poked through the illusion again, the icon was sealed away in the private world of her sex—a different world, a better world. That's what a woman was really for—to smother, if only for a few infrequent moments, the beast that was always gnawing away at a man. He had his nature, she had hers. Filth and purity. You couldn't compromise them, or allow them to mix. When you did, purity was no longer pure, but filth was just as disgusting.

"Where's Allukah?"

"For the love of Shamask," Muskim truckled. "I don't know. Why would I lie to—"

A sharp yank of the chain strangled the rest, holding him that way till his wolfish face turned blue. Then she dropped him and let him grovel.

"Where is Allukah?" Sheryl asked with infinite patience. Glancing at Kio, she turned when she thought he looked back at her.

Allukah!

Sheryl!

What puzzled Kio the most was how these two monsters could be such bitter enemies. Maybe on the outside they were as different as butterflies and beetles, one the most tantalizing vampire, the other the most repulsive. But inside they were identical, polluted to the core of their worm-eaten wombs. Both of them used men. Gluttonous, possessive, they drained the last drop out of a man and still wouldn't let him go because he was still their property, like an old mule or a worn out sock. Roaring across the plains, they plucked and ravished, bit the heart out of the melons and let the rest rot—or pressed them into dry husks like flowers between the pages of a book. These she-devils were so much alike they could be twins. And maybe that was it.

Their greedy rivalry kept them at each other's throat. Both wanted the same thing. Both were too stubborn to give up a man even after they'd sucked the life out of him. Even last night while Allukah had her drooling mouth around Sheryl's breast.

Yes. That was the real answer. Men were just surrogates, substitutes. That's why they always went after the same poor creature. Kio had only been a proxy. When they made their perverted love to his body, they were really making love to each other! Allukah and Sheryl. Lovers! That's what this killing, this torture and maiming, this undiluted insanity was all about. That's why Allukah had stolen the armor, why she had her pet's hair and skin bleached—to look like Sheryl. They were both famished for each other's flesh, as cheap, as common, as disgusting as two bitches in heat. And for that, whole cities, the entire known world had to suffer? Kio turned his head and spit in Sheryl's direction. Now that he'd uncovered her secret, he was glad he was no longer a man.

"Where is Allukah?"

"I don't—" As soon as he felt the tension in the chain increase, Maskim rose on his toes and screamed.

"I hate that goat-faced maggot. Don't you understand? Why would I lie? I've no reason to protect her."

Sighing deeply, Sheryl fluttered her green eyes in Maskim's general direction. he shivered, the sweat spraying off him like water off a wet dog.

"You also have no reason to help me."

Just beyond the crest of the hill, jackals howled while they waited for the Somelon to finish. They'd heard how the hyenas feasted on Lewylln. Now they wanted a turn to come down and pick through the roasted Horlas before the buzzards got away with the best parts. But they were cautious. Sheryl had passed this way before and most of them had limps or scars to prove it.

"No reason. . .except the jackals," Maskim's thick tongue croaked. "If Allukah found out how much I've helped you already, there'd be no place in the world for me to hide. Not even Somelon."

"Somelon!" It was a laugh, but she had to force it out. "The witch would fall apart at the mention of the name. And nobody can find Somelon any more, not even me."

"Allukah has long arms. Longer, even, than yours. She has mentioned Somelon to me. She has been there."

"Nonsense!" A chill ran over her spine and out to her arms, jerking the chain. Maskim jumped off the ground, then crashed back down in a heap.

"I. . ." he choked. "I only repeat what she told me."

"You talk like the fool you are. Allukah is the least of your worries. She's not here now. But I am. You saw what happened to Lewylln."

Maskim looked over to the brown spot on the dirt that was all that was left of the hairless giant.

"You think it will be easy for you to destroy the queen of the Horlas?" Noticing the way Sheryl's eyes kept drifting toward Kio, Maskim started to sway. As he did, he gradually pulled a little slack into the chain. All the while he kept chattering to cover what he was doing.

"Sometimes the dead refuse to stay buried. There are many stories of those who were killed only to return to kill again. Some of those stories are of Somelons."

"For a Somelon," Sheryl answered distractedly. "Nothing is impossible. And I, you fur-bellied fool, am the only Somelon around."

Maskim moved in small circles now, secretly closing the distance between himself and the woman warrior. But his haste made him careless. A length of chain slid through the tail of the brass monkey with a telltale rattle. Sheryl turned on him, pulled the chain tight.

"*Aaaaashhhht!*" The hunchback left the ground and, as quickly, crashed back down.

"Curse your mother's rotten womb!" Maskim spit saliva and blood.

"Your curses bounce off her grave, cretin!"

"Maybe. But some of us, oh warrior, have never died before. Without experience, you can't expect us to do a good job the first time. We have to keep doing it, again and again." He shrugged his hump in Kio's direction. "There's one over there wishes he had a little practice."

Sheryl followed the shrug to the forelorn blue figure crouching in the shade of the aral tree. She was in time to see him spit in her direction. Savagely, her arm tore at the chain in retaliation. She pulled it hard, over and again, dangling Maskim like a spider over a hot griddle. The dirt spouted up in rolling clouds, the village gate swaying, till, finally, her arm grew tired. Maskim came down, smashing his furry face deep into the ground.

"For the last time. Where is Allukah?"

"C-c-c-c-ave." Teeth and blood spurted through holes in his lips.

"You know I trailed her to the Jibway caves before I came here. She wouldn't go back there."

"No!" Maskim gasped, his voice a full octave higher than before. "The Anhatan tunnels where the ghost wagons are buried. That's where she keeps the body of her husband."

"Liar! I played kickball with Micar's head and cremated his flea-bitten body."

"No, no, listen to me. Before. Long ago. Allukah had another man. Your kind of man." The cretin flapped around in the dirt, honking like a seal. "Yes. Yes, a man who knew her before she was a Horla, even

131

before the Najucular stones rotted her away from inside, I tell you. After he died, she stole his body to bring it back to life. I saw her try it. I think she succeeded, only to have him die again when he saw her face."

Unseen behind the hills, the jackals giggled.

"I don't believe it."

"I swear it. I do. I do. And I'll tell you something else because you've been so nice to me. When you find her, be extra careful. She won't be alone."

"Who? Amurti went with her?"

"Not her son. A daughter."

"A daughter?" A smile curled on Sheryl's lips. She didn't know if she believed him or not. But she wanted to. "Good. Very good. I can't leave her an orphan, so I'll kill her first—while her mother watches."

"Again, I warn you, Somelon, because I like you. You may very well put an end to all our misery by killing Allukah. But if you do, her daughter will stalk you. From that day on, you'll know no peace. Even the walls of Somelon, could you find them, won't be thick enough to protect you. You can't battle against Allukah's daughter anymore than you can snatch your reflection in a mirror."

"I will kill her. I swear it. Or die trying."

"Your vow is your own death warrant, Somelon."

"Enough. I have no time for riddles, trickster."

The woman warrior jumped to her feet. She pulled off her robe, threw it across the couch and knelt to gather her armor while the prisoner looked on panting. Some cravings are strong enough to blot out any pain and Maskim was as craven as sin itself.

"It is against my better judgment, you understand." The cretin gulped. "But I'm willing to lead you to her. You won't find her by yourself."

"You?" Sheryl spoke absently, inspecting her gear.

"Yes, me. I'll wait outside the tunnels, guard the horses and all. You know. After you kill her, you can tell me all about it. We'll have a good laugh about it together, a jug of wine and some you know what."

"I thought you didn't want me to kill her. And then there's her daughter. Aren't you afraid?" Sheryl wriggled into her chemise.

"Maskim is afraid of nothing. Her daugher is putty in my hands, I tell you. And look how useful I've been to you already. I brought you here without anyone knowing, mixed you in with the dancers."

"You were well paid. What is your price this time?"

Maskim's answer was to run his weaselly eyes up her body from her bare toes to her face, then back down again, stopping halfway while his mouth drooled.

"I see." She placed a hand on her stomach and looked to the still figure in the shade of the aral tree. "Thank you, Maskim. But I already have company."

"Him?" The cretin's mouth dropped open. "He hates you. And what good is he now, after what Lewylln did to him? His dagger is bent for good."

"Only a halfwit could think that a few inches of hard flesh could transform a pig into a prince."

"I may only have half my wits, but I have all my man parts."

Sheryl took a step toward him. Her great body radiated so brilliantly it blinded the floundering cretin.

Maskim squinted, taking in the full glow of her charms. Even through all that hair on his face, you could see him smile at what he saw.

"I'll be good for you, I swear. Better than you've ever had before." Eagerly, he bunched his words together in stuttering packets. "You'll see. I know I'm not good to look at, but you can always close your eyes. And I last.

God, do I last. I have endurance, you know? I don't quit. And I'm as horny as a ram. All you want. Anytime you want."

Maskim worked his twisted body up to its knees. With his arms tied to his side, it was a struggle peppered with many grunts and curses, but his avid smile wilted when he looked up at her again.

"What're you doing?" A cloud seemed to roll across his face, eclipsing the brightness.

Sheryl reeled in the chain, pulling Maskim the rest of the way to his feet. Then she drove a stake through the links into the ground, holding him fast.

"Do you think my brain is as scrambled as yours? The minute I let you go you'd scuttle off to warn her or try and sell my trail to Amurti or some other Horla dog. I want no interference."

"But you owe me, Somelon. I snuck you into the Great Hut last night, just like you wanted."

"I wanted Allukah. I didn't get her."

"Is that my fault?"

"If I knew for sure. . ." Her face tightened, though she shook it right off. "You helped me for the silver I gave you, and because you wanted to see them all punished for the way they treated you. You played a good trick on the Horlas. I won't give you the chance to play one on me."

"I told you where Allukah is. You have to let me go. You owe me."

"You're right." Sheryl stared down with those glowing green eyes of hers. "I owe you something for your information. So I won't kill you."

She started to walk away.

"But the jackals!" Maskim cried, scouring the crest of the hills. He couldn't see anything, though he thought he still heard them chuckling.

"Oh, yes, the jackals. How silly of me." Sheryl bent over to scoop a knife off the ground. It was a tiny dagger, its handle cast in the shape of a deer's foot. "This is for you and your information."

She threw it. The blade struck into the ground between Maskim's clubbed feet.

"Maybe it's not as long as the precious dagger you swear you have hidden in your pants. Still, you'll probably find it more effective on them than yours was on me. It'll take you a while to work the knife up to your hands, though I'm sure a real man like yourself— a whole man with all his man parts—will do it without working up a sweat—especially after the first jackal pokes his snout over the hill."

Sheryl busied herself now, strapping on her armor, pulling on her fur boots. Her sword was still clean, never having left its sheath, and her helmet shone. When she came to her war club fashioned from the lightning-struck limb of the walnut tree that had snatched her life away from the sun, Sheryl rubbed her palm across the Somelon face carved into its shaft. Raising it to her mouth, she kissed it once again, before hanging the club from her belt.

"You can't leave me here!" Maskim crowed, all his guile leaking out with the beads of sweat that suddenly began soaking through his forehead. "I have. . .I have more to tell you, Somelon. About Allukah. About. . . about her daughter. I know things that will pierce your armored breast like a crossbow bolt and tear out your heart. Listen to me. I know. Allukah's daughter is. . ."

Sheryl pulled the chain one link tighter and Maskim's desperate melody turned into garbled nonsense.

"You'll stay here, cinder-brain. The knife will reach your stubby fingers before we leave the camp. Then you can tickle the jackals with it while you tell them all those

135

things you know. Try and make them listen to the song of your blade. That would be the way a halfwit fights. But if you're smart, you'll use the knife on yourself."

With that, Sheryl drew a deep breath and turned to face Kio.

Chapter 12

A Wounded Bird

When she came close enough, the pungent scent of the aral tree masked the smell of burnt flesh that was baked into the air.

"Kio. It's time for us to leave this place." Her voice bubbled up and burst. There wasn't any way to control it, so she kept from looking into his face. Instead, she fooled with one of the shoulder straps of her armor, buckling it, unbuckling it, pulling it so tight it cut deep into her skin.

Towering over Kio, Sheryl stood between that small, huddled man and the sun. Her hair was a golden, glowing cloud that intercepted all the light and scattered it before it reached him, so Kio lay in a deepened shadow. Still, no shadow ever cast was deep enough to compete against the black pit trapping his soul at this moment. Sheryl was strong. She was always strong, even as she slept, even when she loved. But at this, the lowest point in Kio's life, the very thing he didn't need was her strength.

A tough, healthy, energetic woman was more than useless to him. What this weak man really needed was someone to be weaker than him, someone vulnerable who could bend a little and absorb some of the shock, who could take a full share of his agony and writhe by his side, gnashing her teeth, tearing her garments, and take his mind off himself. More than anything, Kio needed not to suffer alone. The burden on his mind was an overloaded voltage sizzling across his nervous system. If some other mind didn't shunt off some of the voltage, if some other bundle of synapses didn't tap off some of the current, Kio would short circuit. He'd simply explode.

"Listen to me, Kio. We have to go. Now."

Wings flapped behind her as vultures, their naked necks arching, fought over the bodies of the Horlas. There was more than enough to go around, yet some only wanted what some other beak already had.

Sheryl peeked out of the corner of her eyes as she knelt down to straighten one of her silver shin guards. Though Kio's face was still in the shadows, his eyes were bright, discharging an orange light when they turned on her, growing hotter than any of the embers still smoldering in the ruins of the Great Hut. Beneath them, his smooth jaw was set hard.

"Go? I'm not going anywhere. Don't you know that? There's nowhere for me to go." He was daring her to contradict him.

"We can't stay here."

"You're free to go whenever you like. I don't see any walls to keep you. You burned them all down, haven't you? Sure you haven't missed any? You might have overlooked a stray old woman who might still be breathing, or maybe a baby that hasn't been crushed."

Sheryl's hand rested on her hip. Through the warrior's arm, Kio could see Maskim struggling to work the dagger up to his fingers while he dangled from the chain. Maddeningly, the blade kept slipping between his toes and back to the ground.

"Oh, there's one that's still alive. I think I'll stay here and talk over old times with the cretin till death comes around to claim him. Who knows, maybe the old reaper will take me along too."

"The only one who's going to die is Allukah."

The unexpected sound of that name chased Kio's glowing eyes so deep into his skull the sockets looked empty. The small body clenched itself into a ball like a startled hedgehog. He hugged his knees to his chest, shivered so violently Sheryl forgot herself and rushed to his side. As she moved, her armor clinked with a sound duller than the light finger cymbals she used last night as she danced.

"Don't be frightened, Kio. Not now. There's no need for it. Nobody'll ever hurt you again. I promise. I'll put that Horla sow in her grave—forever."

Her quick movements, the way she talked in bursts, only drove him deeper inside himself, so deep the trembling stopped and his body went limp. His breathing turned so shallow you could hardly notice it, even if you looked for it, and Sheryl had to hold back her hand to keep from touching him to see if he was still alive.

Promises would do no good now. They would only make things worse. The wounds in Kio's ego had clotted, but they were far from healed and any mention of what would never be allowed to happen again, only made the memory of what had happened more vivid. He stayed a prisoner of the past, shackled to images of Allukah as securely as Maskim was chained to the gate.

"Kio, I brought your robe, the one I bought for you in the bazaar." Sheryl's hand dipped into her bag and came out with a stream of red and green cloth. "I feel it's a symbol of our love the way you—"

"Our love is back in that cave chained to a table, its guts spilled out on the cold stone."

Yes, Kio was trapped by his memory, and like a fox that gnaws off its own leg when its foot is caught, he struggled to free himself, to leave it all behind him, everything, good and bad, Allukah and Sheryl.

"It was the Pursangs that died, Kio. They paid for their crime with their lives."

"Of course. That's the only price Somelons know. There's no in between. Good or bad, live or die."

"That's as it should be."

"Then why do I always get the bad? Why is everything always dead after you leave? Where's the good? Where's the life?"

"I didn't make the world, Kio. Things are as they are. If it weren't for Somelons, there would be no world except the Horlas. You know that."

"Maybe it would be better that way."

"Now I know you're sick. Your mouth moves. It makes sounds, all right, but not much sense." She bent down and draped the robe across his lap. She wanted to keep doing something, anything, to prevent his mind from circling back.

"I saved it for you. Put it on, Kio."

He didn't lift a finger. The robe lay limp, running across his body like paint that had been spilled long ago and dried, only moving when the wind caught the hem and swept it up as though looking for something underneath it, something that had been lost or misplaced.

"Maybe you'd rather eat something first. You can't say food is your enemy, at least. It's always been good to you."

Peeling back the mouth of a silk purse, she took Kio's hand and filled the palm with tiny brown triangles. These were eagles' tongues, a special concoction, dried, soaked in wine, rolled in a secret recipe of peppered paste that titillated the male palate. They were especially prized by male warriors who knew no better. They were not, however, the food of strength and normally Sheryl would have passed right over them when she looted Micar's tent, had not the sight of the bag reminded her instantly of Kio. So she took them for a present.

Kio stubbornly refused to respond and the eagles' tongues lay undisturbed on his palm till she grabbed hold of his shoulder and held one of the treats beneath his nose. His nostrils twitched. The muscles of his jaw slackened enough for her to force the tiny wedge into his mouth.

Kio chewed one. Again, aimlessly as a cow, till the taste cracked through to his tongue. Then his mouth puckered and the eagles' tongue came flying out. He flung the rest into her face. Sheryl kept her hand tight on his shoulder. Maybe too tight, for Kio winced noticeably.

"That's a warrior's food and I'm no warrior. I'm not fit to eat it."

"Food doesn't know who eats it." She was shaking his shoulder now. "It doesn't care if it fills the stomach of a lizard or a lion—or just the kind of fool you're being, Kio."

"When I was a man, I was not foolish. I'm no longer a man."

"A man! You say the word like it meant you'd been a god. Are the Horlas men? Is that what you want to be? Is it the body that makes the man—or his spirit?"

"I haven't either." Kio kept talking as though he resented her intrusion into his thoughts. He had everything worked out so neatly before, had every block in place, and now she was rocking that tower of logic, threatening to topple it. "When I'm hungry, I'll slosh in the pen with swine. When I'm cold, I'll roll up in the ashes with the corpses. I better get used to it."

"You'll go with me, that's where you'll go. Stop feeling sorry for yourself." Sheryl released his shoulder, though she couldn't resist giving him a slight shove that knocked him back against the tree.

"I'm not strong enough to stop you."

Forcing his face toward hers, her fingers left streaks in the black soot particles covering his cheeks.

"It can't be all that bad, Kio." Shifting the striped robe from his lap, she peeked under the edge of the blue cloak. "Let me see what they did."

"No!" The scream that came out of his mouth froze the vultures in the sky. His fist flew up into her face, then he threw the robe after it.

Sheryl fell back with the red and green robe over her head. She was stunned, not so much by the force of the blow as by the hate behind it. Kio had struck her. He'd tried to hurt her. Whether or not he succeeded was unimportant. But again she told herself he was sick, hurt, not responsible. She swallowed hard, took the robe off her head, and leaned toward him.

"Kio, you know it makes no difference to me if you're—"

"Who do you think you're kidding? No difference. You'd say anything to get your pet monkey to go along with you now, because he's your property. But in a week you'll be bouncing off the walls looking for a man. You'll claw at yourself while every concavity in your body cries out for a convex hunk of flesh to fill it. Then you'll start hating me. Well don't bother because this time I win, Somelon. This time I fooled you good because I already started hating you. And that makes me immune to you. There's no way for you to hurt me."

"Kio!" She was pleading, though it sounded so unnatural coming from her mouth. "In Somelon there are mystics and alchemists. The Magi of Maluchus owe my father many favors. I'll take you to all of them. They'll make you right again. I promise."

"More promises? You hand them out pretty freely.

Well you can't change what's happened. I trusted you once. Now look at me.''

Sheryl seized the hand he was waving in her face and jammed it down the neck of her armor breastplate. His fingers recognized the skin instantly. They trembled, working their way deeper, over her breast as they searched for the swollen nipple that was there someplace waiting. The fingers squirmed right. They wriggled left. But it was no good. With a squeal of frustration, Kio ripped his hand out. Spinning around, he buried his face in the roots of the aral tree. He wept.

Very slowly, Sheryl rose to her feet and began folding the red and green robe. When she put it back into her bag, she shivered, trying to shake away the contempt that was circling around the edges of her grief. Was this wretched, sobbing body really the same Kio she had known those nights in Centropolis? An image of a bird fluttered through her mind, a muddy starling beating a broken wing against the forest floor. Unable to fly away from danger, to leave its fear on the ground far below, the bird scrambled madly, peeping. In its frenzy it was tearing itself apart. Smothering the wounded bird might be an act of mercy that went beyond love. This bird had suffered so much since the caravan, though every Somelon learned early that there is nothing so bad it should make you afraid to go on living. Her mother had said that to her many times. Compared with the trials Sheryl weathered every day, Kio's troubles seemed insignificant. Yet Kio was a male, a member of the weaker sex by the accident of his birth. He was not a Somelon. And no man could possibly have done to Sheryl what Allukah had done to Kio.

No. Sheryl set her jaw. No matter what, she wasn't ready to let contempt drive a wedge between them. Not yet. She'd bind the wounded bird's wing. She'd nurse him back to health, keep him from destroying himself. After that, there'd be plenty of time to decide what she really felt for him.

"You'll come with me." She swirled a green cape around her shoulders, fastening it to her breastplate. "It's a two day journey to the Anhatan tunnels and Allukah won't wait forever."

"Allukah! Allukah!" Kio wailed. "You're two of a kind, you and that damned Allukah, born from the same rotten egg. You use me like a rag doll, throwing me back and forth till the stuffing leaks out."

He drove his head into the dirt, covering it with leaves as though he could hide himself from the two demons. His tears turned the dirt to mud.

"I wish I never laid eyes on you, Sheryl."

"It is as you say, Kio." The hesitation had left her voice completely. "You can't change what has happened. All we can is go on into tomorrow—where we'll find Allukah waiting for us."

Stooping, she grabbed an arm and pulled him to his feet. Kio wobbled, then leaned back limp against the tree trunk. Pawing at his smudged cheeks, the wounded bird surveyed the ruins of the Horla camp through muddy tears, passing over the burnt-out anthill that once had been the Great Hut. Flies circled around his head.

"I'll go with you," he sobbed. "I'll go to. . .to that place. If Allukah. . .if she kills you, I guess I'll die too. That's as it should be. If you kill her. . .well, I'll go with you to the tunnels, but I will go no further."

They rode out of the ashes together. Kio let his pony trail a few hoof beats behind the white stallion without even taking the trouble to hold the reins, and his head bobbed like a balloon at the end of a stick.

Their leaving left a vacuum in the camp, one that

drew every jackal and scavenger out of the surrounding hills. Before the silent riders were out of sight, Maskim's screams came rolling over their shoulders pursued by growls and snarling snaps. Neither rider turned around, and it wasn't long before the screaming stopped.

A gloating sun kept pace with the travelers. Shamask beamed. Though he'd personally been powerless to stop the haughty Somelon, it looked to him as though this tiny, shriveled man on the ragged pony might just be the one to bring the blonde giant to her knees. So as the mounts stepped onto the dry lava beds, Shamask surrounded the trudging silhouettes with a crimson nimbus.

Unshod hooves beat hollow notes out of the lava, for there were many tiny bubbles trapped inside when the rock cooled. It was along these sloping banks that the nymphs once frolicked, slipping through rolling white water while they teased men with their slim, childish bodies. All their sweet revels ended the day Leemartiff stepped out of the forest and found them spread out like candy before his hungry eyes.

Leemartiff, the mortal husband of the wood goddess Gueva, never needed much of an excuse to pander and one casual smile from the nymphs had been enough to make him plunge into the river where, trying to grab and hold on to the slippery-skinned ondives, he drowned. To punish the sirens, the grieving Gueva turned the rolling waters into bubbling magma that trapped and cremated every last nymph. Now Sheryl dismounted to lead the stallion and the pony over the crystallized beds, careful to keep their hooves out of the holes where girlish bodies had turned into the dust that still rode the winds bringing tears to travelers' eyes.

The first centaur wasn't sighted till late afternoon, yet

once word spread, the bushes bloomed with these man-horse creatures. Centaurs have always been known to favor Somelons and though they lead somewhat dissolute lives (centaurs knowing little about such supposed virtues as temperance and self-control), a code of chivalry has evolved which binds them to the service of the women warriors. It's a fealty the centaurs relish and they would have prostrated themselves before Sheryl if they hadn't realized she was on a special errand, one that admitted no allies—one she had to carry out alone. So, once they satisfied their curiosity by ogling the golden warrior and her odd squire, they disappeared back into the brush as secretly as they came.

The table of the five colossi was deserted when the two silent riders passed that way. With chairs pushed back or overturned, and empty goblets, smashed plates strewn around the countryside, there'd be no feasting there that day. Sheryl and her sullen companion rode between the granite columns that were the legs of this massive set of furniture, their hoofbeats echoing off the underside of the table forty feet above their heads. When they reappeared out of the cool shadows, Shamask was waiting, shining.

When they passed the Poko cliffs, Sheryl stood up in the stirrups, but when she shaded her eyes she didn't see any of the Rocs roosting in their nests. Only the broken shells from which the fledglings of the giant birds hatched littered the matted floors of straw and twigs, so Sheryl didn't bother to point them out to Kio.

When at last the earth took pity on this harassed couple and rolled them out of range of the gloating solar disk, Sheryl pulled rein, stopping so Kio might rest. She took fire out of her bag and they sat crosslegged on opposite sides of the flames, cradling their chests in their arms. Sheryl tood dried pomance from her saddlebags, but he shook his head when it was offered to him. Nor did he drink any of the aral-root wine, even though it was real wine, not the cloudy Horla swill. Sheryl ate alone. She was a warrior who couldn't afford the luxury of starving herself out of spite.

Both of them were too stubborn to surrender to the fatigue that had a strangle hold on their bodies. Feeding peat and branches into the fire, they stayed awake far into the night, stoking the flames until a bonfire burned between them that was every bit as bright as the fires burning inside their chests—the fires only Allukah's blood could extinguish.

Outside the reach of the light, the stallion snorted, the pony whinnied. Freed from their harnesses, they rubbed their long-maned necks together. And in the black darkness a cross between a white Somelon stallion and a painted Horla pony was conceived.

There was never any doubt that Kio would be the first to collapse, and as soon as he tottered Sheryl crept over to cover him with a yak-skin blanket, then cradled his head in her lap. That's when, as she ran her fingers through the tangle of hair, she discovered the Horlas had taken his right ear.

"My poor little bird," she cooed, touching her lips to the place where the ear had been.

Kio was not fully conscious at that moment. He wasn't asleep either. But he didn't stir or let on he knew what she was doing, though it was the first time he allowed himself to admit that part of his fear was for her, that he might never see her again. They were together now, for better or worse. Maybe they should just let Allukah go, ride out in the opposite direction as soon as it was light. But no. Kio knew only too well that it was impossible. They couldn't leave Allukah to be an open question between them. He also knew Allukah wouldn't be the end of it. Unless they died, there would always be something—Horlas, Pursangs, dragons or magicians—something would always be shoving between them, driving them apart. There was always a question calling for a Somelon to settle it. There would always be something to lure her away, and someday that something might keep her from coming back.

But Kio said none of these things to her.

All through the night Shamask, afraid he'd miss a crucial part of the emotional carnage in this battle of the sexes, raced around the globe. Before his shining forehead crested the horizon, Sheryl crept back to her side of the fire and preserved what was left of Kio's pride by pretending to be asleep.

Shivering in the morning mist, they saddled and bridled their mounts silently. The way the animals insisted on standing together kept warrior and sculptor on opposite sides, but when they chanced to put their feet in the stirrups and swung their two bodies over the horses' flanks, their eyes met. For an instant their two bodies hung there in space, eyes locked till the pony, for no reason, took a bite out of the stallion's rump. He bolted, breaking the connection between their eyes.

A long plume of smoke rising across their path wasn't a dust devil but a caravan, a long line of squeaking, clanking Teutite wagons. As Sheryl and Kio neared, the plume suddenly billowed, then twisted as the drivers whipped the oxen into a lumbering run.

"They think we're Horlas," Sheryl pointed. "They're afraid we'll murder and rob them."

"The fools! Don't they know Somelons aren't thieves? They only kill for sport."

So those words were the last to pass between them till after they sighted the Anhatan mounds.

At dusk, from high atop the palisades, the warrior looked down to the Tent River which already glowed pale green from the fish whose transparent bodies gave a clear view of their writhing luminous skeletons. Just beyond the white-capped waters the Anhatan mounds were cut by harsh shadows in the dying light. It was an island graveyard marked by sheer, windowed tombstones piled one atop the other and sparkling with red stains. They say a city had been there once, before the Mushroom Wars and the reign of fire pulled the spires out of the sky's eye. Long ago the steel skeletons of these structures had rusted away. The stone crumbled, wedging into massive, hollow mounds like the surface of some exotic crystal studded with facets and pockets. Beneath the mounds ran a system of tunnels, mile after pitch-black mile of tunnels, weaving, intersecting, threading through the skin of the earth like the nests of some long-extinct ants. Somewhere in those tunnels, if Maskim had told the truth, they would find Allukah, and maybe her daughter, a creature beyond human imagination. It was also possible that somewhere in those tunnels Sheryl and Kio would find their deaths.

The warrior looked up the river to the concrete willow trees with steel branches that were planted in the center of the river's flow. Once a bridge had spanned the chasm, but now the only way across was through the cold, racing currents.

Sheryl dug spurred heels into the flanks of the stallion. Pebbles, then rocks, crumbled beneath its inching hooves as she urged the beast over the edge of the sheer palisades. With nothing but sky between them and the water, they hurled down into the river with a splash.

Kio didn't have to whip the pony. She wasn't about to let the stallion leave her behind now. So when Sheryl resurfaced, she heard them splashing into the river behind her.

Chapter 13

Beneath the Anhatan Mounds

Once across the Tent River, a drenched Somelon slid out of her saddle to loosen the cinch strap and peel the bridle off the stallion's head. Kio did the same to his pony. They'd go on foot from this point since the crumbling concrete mounds could easily snap the brittle legs of the animals as though they were dried blades of grass. And there was always the chance that Sheryl and Kio would not return.

The animals were delighted to run free. And they ran together along the shallow beach with the pony prancing in the lead, teasing, nipping, staying just beyond the reach of the snorting stallion.

Climbing inward, away from the river, the two searchers were dried by the rising evening winds. As the sun peaked over their shadows, they felt for handholds to pull themselves up toward the sky, inching to the summit of one mound, only to have to let themselves down the other side, into valleys where shadows were thick.

The tunnels beneath the Anhatan mounds had many entrances. At even intervals, flights of slippery stairs disappeared into the ground where the light couldn't follow, and Allukah might have been swallowed by any one of them. But Sheryl didn't believe that. So each time they climbed into one of those valleys and found an entrance wide open and waiting like a Malubite whore,

Sheryl walked right by it to the next mound and started climbing again.

The sharp stones cut at their hands, slit the soles of their feet till each grip of Kio's hand left a palmprint, each step a footprint. But they kept on climbing, up one mound, down the next, passing entrance after entrance without even bothering to look inside.

"Here!" Sheryl halted. It was sunset.

Puzzled, Kio looked around. The feet of four separate mounds met here in this hollow, though except for a huge block of granite that had toppled as low as it could go, the place looked no different than any of the countless other hollows they'd passed through without breaking stride. And Sheryl didn't seem much interested in the stone block resting on the black tarmac. Instead, she shifted around in the rubble of surrounding mounds, digging out sharp rocks, discarding some after a quick examination. Eventually she settled on a wedge-shaped chunk and a large, flat stone that fit her hand comfortably. Only then did the approach the granite block.

The coarse grains of the tarmac grated under her armor shin guards as she knelt down. Sliding the wedge into the thin groove between the block and the ground, she covered it with her green cape and began pounding it with the other stone. Kio watched as the granite rose a few inches under the muffled force of the wedge. Placing a flat rock beneath the rock for support, she worked the wedge free. Another rock beneath the wedge, another series of blows, and the rock rose a few more inches. She repeated the technique, over and over till the monolith canted two feet off the ground. When it was high enough, Kio saw a flight of stairs, identical to all the others they'd seen, running down into the earth. Shamask's last rays of light slipped into the rectangular hole to strike a handrail with green paint, the brass shining through like cracks in a furnace wall.

"She isn't in there," Kio backed away from the entrance. "We're wasting our time."

"Time? Do you have someplace else to go, Kio, that you're in such a hurry?"

He glared at her the way men had glared at her before, searching for some sign of weakness, knowing all the while there wasn't the slightest chance he'd find it. After the work of lifting a hundred ton block of stone, she was coated with a thin layer of sweat, and as she turned to face the entrance, her skin flashed brighter than her silver armor. Stooping to crawl inside, she paused.

"Coming?"

Eyes rapidly glazing as he started to back away, Kio stared into the waiting mouth of the entrance and saw instead that other cave with its circling passages, its chains and stone table—and Allukah. Most of all he saw Allukah. Kio stared into the waiting mouth of the entrance and saw that other mouth, that mouth with the broken teeth, the mustache—coming toward him, ready to swallow. His thin legs twitched under his robe, ready to run.

"Kio," Sheryl yelled. "Stop it. There's nothing to be afraid of. Inside this hole we'll find the solution to our problems. It's the only way. These tunnels hold—"

A groan came out of the earth, a long resonant grunt that circled around Sheryl's helmeted head before it spread up into the sky.

"Those tunnels will lead us to our deaths, that's what they'll do." Sweat started leaking on his forehead even though he'd done no work and the air caught between the mounds was cool and still.

"There are worse things than death, Kio."

But it was no good. He didn't budge until another groan broke out of the tunnel and chased him around to the other side of the granite block where he hid.

"Then stay here, Kio, where you'll be safe till I come back for you."

Crawling all the way in, Sheryl was swallowed by the darkness.

Though she couldn't see more than a foot in any direction, the groaning led her on. Her hand, feeling the way along tiled walls, splashed through water trickling out of cracks that ran back as far as the river. Somewhere below, stagnant pools gulped down the fresh water and turned it foul. The cold air crept out of hiding and like an icy palm reached under her armor, under her leather skirt, to wipe away that layer of sweat from her skin. She shuddered, her fur boots spongy as she took another step down. The groans strung together into a howl like a devil dog guarding the gates of hell, then rolled into a whistling banshee calling for her soul.

At the bottom of the stairs the concrete leveled out, though an iron gate stretched parallel to the walls. Sheryl walked along its length till she found a place where she could squeeze through the bars.

It came out of nowhere, a high-pitched, rusty screech like an ungreased axle spinning broken spokes into her head, knocking her winged helmet to the floor. The thing snarled itself in her hair, struggling, tearing at the roots before Sheryl could reach up to grab it. Then those needly teeth pierced her fingers. She snatched at the small, flapping body, twisting around, stumbling, till her feet tripped over something hard, and that something and Sheryl crashed to the concrete. The creature screamed. It beat its wings against her face. Then it was gone.

The warrior held her breath. The racket should have

warned Allukah and robbed Sheryl of the advantage of surprise. Yet the groaning, the deep mellow moaning, whatever its source, went on unchanged. Maybe it had been loud enough to mask the noise.

From where she lay, the entrance through which she'd come was only a pinhole, a distant planet on which Kio lived, unreachable, a million miles away. He was right to have stayed there. He'd be no help to her the way he was. Though Sheryl couldn't help but believe that it would do him a world of good to watch Allukah die.

This stumbling around in the dark had had its chance. It was a bad idea from the start, so Sheryl took fire out of her bag to make a torch, doing her best to shield it and direct the light only in the direction she wanted to go. The thing that had tripped her turned out to be a suitcase that looked as if an angry ape had flung it around a cage for the better part of its existence. When her fingers touched the wrinkled, gray surface, the case tinkled, metallic, like swords. On one side there was a handle and two monogrammed clasps—FFM. Sheryl pressed one. It popped up. She pressed the other and the case sprung open as wide as a hungry clam. Instead of pearls, silverware lined the inside of the synthetic shells. There were spoons—tablespoons, demitasse spoons, serving spoons—knives—butter knives, steak knives—forks and so on. Some were ornate, filigreed or thick with a black sulfate tarnish, while others were cheap aluminum or stainless steel. They must have come from a dozen different places.

Mixed in with the flatware were the threads of a few towels long since disintegrated, a few loose house bricks, and an assortment of vials. One was a glass bottle plugged with a rotating ball, another a plastic tube that sprayed when she squeezed it. The contents had evaporated decades ago, though a trace of the scent still lingered, a spray cologne manufactured in an ancient world. It burned Sheryl's nose. She sneezed.

Raising the torch over her bare head, she spied another, briefer case. The brittle skin of a prehistoric animal covered both sides. From its handle, a chain linked out to a single handcuff. Inside the clasped ring was a bone. Judging by the long tapered looks of it, the bone had once been a forearm, though it was impossible to tell for sure since it was hacked away about where the elbow would have been. Sheryl concluded it was a prisoner's arm, for the case held only green dust and who, except a criminal being punished, would be chained to a case of green dust?

Pushing the case aside, Sheryl climbed to her feet. She wasn't an archeologist or a theologian and the problems of the past, especially in that inaccessible era before the Mushroom War, were of no interest to her. Time had taken care of all those problems, found a permanent, irrevocable solution by killing off everyone who knew what the problems were. Yes, time would take care of Sheryl's problems too, if she let it. But Sheryl wasn't the kind to wait around for time. In her world, Somelons did the things time could not or would not do.

As soon as she moved, a light flashed just to her right. Stepping back, she crouched, clutching for the handle of her sword. But the light was gone. Sheryl stretched out the dripping torch. The light flashed again and Sheryl saw her reflection in a small mirror attached to a metal machine with a row of small knobs and rectangular windows. Her hair was damp, hanging in strings to her shoulders which were smudged with the same slimy mold that covered the floor and made it so slippery. She'd lost her helmet, though her sword still waited in its scabbard and the war club hung from her belt. Leaving the mirror behind, the warrior went deeper into the darkness.

She found the ghost wagons where they had always stood, their wheels rusted to the rails at the bottom of a concrete trough. Through the grimy windows, Sheryl caught a quick glimpse of the skeletons still sitting upright in their seats. From here the tunnels ran out in all directions like a sudden explosion of blackness. Once the ghost wagons had rumbled through them, chasing their future, their horns blaring like pterodactyls, though long ago the rest of the rails had been stolen to be beaten into swords and now the only sound was the moaning.

She kept following the noise and the further she went, the louder it became, its hollow echo making the darkness darker. Sheryl followed the noise. There was never any doubt about which way to go. Especially after the bodies started to appear.

At first they were only piles of bones, small and scattered, then gradually growing larger, thicker. They could have been any age—as old as the frozen ghosts in the green wagons, or as recent as the massacre of the Teutite caravan. You couldn't tell with bones. As she went deeper, some of the skeletons wore belts, sandals, a strip of old cloth, then bits of dried flesh could be seen clinging to the bones. Shriveled into mummies, the corpses released a noxious, choking odor.

It didn't take the warrior long to figure out where she was. This vault was Allukah's museum, a putrifying display of twenty years of tragedy, of torture and waste as pet after pet surrendered its life to a Horla's terrible appetite. Sheryl wondered which one of these had been Allukah's husband, the first one, before Micar. Maybe, as Maskim had suggested, she'd really brought the dead man back from the grave. Or was that just another one of the riddles cretins like to pose—like the phantom daughter of Allukah. Sheryl knew that, like most fools, nothing Maskim said was fully false—or fully true. It was a question of half answers, pieces of a puzzle selected at random, but all fitting together once you had the key. Maskim had told her Allukah was here. Sheryl had found the tunnel. She could only hope now that she'd find Allukah waiting at the other end.

The corpses turned still fresher. the Somelon could begin to identify the sexes, even the way they'd died. Propped against the tile walls, or lounging on the wet concrete with wispy beards of gray mold ringing their faces, their eyes were all open, though most of the sockets were empty. With the moaning chant clinging to the air as heavy as incense, it was like stepping into a medieval cathedral.

The women had their breasts sliced off. Maybe Allukah had been jealous of anything that made them more woman than she could ever be. The men were disemboweled. True to character, the Horla bitch was never satisfied. After draining them dry, she still wanted more. She knew they were holding out on her, that somewhere inside a drop of hormones, a dram of semen still lay hidden in a fatty sac or moist membrane. Allukah wanted it all. And she'd gone after it.

Sheryl looked back again the way she had come. The light from the entrance was gone. It was good Kio hadn't seen this.

Somelon eyes swelled big as a cat's, soaking up the weak light, then squeezing the images out of it. All around her the darkness sparkled with the eyes of rats and bats, the creatures most at home in the tunnels of Allukah, the witnesses to her crimes. They blinked in time with the moaning and as the cries came quicker, deeper, suffocating on their own breath, Sheryl began to make out words in the ragged, coughing rhythms.

"Good. Yes. Still good. Still. The best."

Here the tunnel took a sharp turn. Sheryl approached it carefully, hugging the wall and peeking around the corner. She saw light ahead. On the far tile wall it projected a large silhouette, a black body riding a strange beast she couldn't see. The arms of the figure curled wildly over its head. Hair mushroomed out, whipping back and forth with each twist. And through it all came the groans, the muttering words between.

"You know. . .how. To drive me mad. Oh—oh, yes. You know, you devil. Better than all of them. Every one of them. No one as good. As you. All of them. I tried all of them. But you. Oh. My love. You are the best. The longest. You. . ."

Creeping closer, her ears stuffed full of the grunting chant, Sheryl grabbed the corner of the wall with both hands and flung her body around it. Flying into the chamber she found Allukah.

Sheryl shrank back as soon as she saw the Horla queen, not out of fear, but from shock. The sight was almost too much for even a Somelon's brain to absorb. Allukah hadn't noticed her yet. Her cloudy eyes didn't see anything except maybe an occasional glimpse of the ceiling through fluttering eyelids as she thrashed and bounced. It was her body that cast the silhouette, her throat that gargled out the groans, as she rode the mummified shaft of a corpse!

"You can't see me now," she sung. "You don't know how. . .how ugly I've grown. But I've learned so much. . .so very much. I've tried them all. Oh, yes, yes. I know you're the only one. I've always known. The best. So good! Even better than before she came and spoiled it all."

Up and down she went, smashing into the stone table as she rode the dead body. With only a leather belt pulled tight into her bulging skin, her hands groped along her chest, wringing her breasts, then fluttered up to her bubbling, mustache-fringed lips. A finger slipped inside. Another. She licked them, bit at the knuckles. Saliva leaked out in long, stretching globs to coat the quivering feet of the corpse. And all the while the groans went on without a break.

Sheryl's stomach lurched. One hand clutched for her sword while the other juggled the torch trying to hold on. Forcing her body to go forward, she stood directly in front of the stone table and waited for Allukah's wandering eyes to settle on her.

The Horla queen had hypnotized herself with the frantic, jerking rhythms of her own body. Oblivious to everything else, she churned faster, ever faster, becoming a single, giant lump of shimmering suet. Then her eyes flew open. She saw Sheryl.

Allukah didn't stop. She couldn't now. She'd gone too far, was so close she could only go faster, riding after the climax with desperate lunges. Faster. Still faster. She screamed. "Sheryl! Not now. No! Not again!" A speck of green exploded in those cloudy eyes.

Sheryl saw the orgasm clustering. She wasn't going to let it happen. So she thrust the torch into that wild face.

Allukah's arms, her legs shot out like a star. She tumbled backward, away from the flame, rolling off the table, her hair blazing. Yet even when her head bounced against the concrete, her body didn't miss a beat. It went on pumping as though it might somehow still reach the summit. But it wasn't any good. It was gone in a flash, just like her hair. She'd never reach it now. And if Sheryl had her way, the Horla queen would never shiver with the ecstacy of an orgasm again.

Pulling out her sword, Sheryl sliced away the mummified male organ that still poked up into the air like a stale salami. Allukah cried out as if she were the one cut by the blade. On the return swing, Sheryl caught the brown flesh with the flat of the sword and batted it to Allukah.

"Here. Finish the job by hand, you freak. One last poke, and then my sword."

Allukah leaped into the dust, but instead of the severed digit she came up with a sword. She whipped it high over her smoking head, but even as she gripped the long, smooth handle, you could see her regret that Sheryl hadn't come a few minutes later.

"You ruined him!" Slapping her fat feet on the ground, Allukah bared her crooked teeth. "My husband. The only thing I had left. You had to take him away. Didn't you?"

"As you ruined Kio. But Kio's still alive. He'll heal as soon as I get rid of you."

"Kio?" Those cloudy eyes swirled as her mind raced back to this world from wherever they'd been. "The whelp? You won't get anything out of him. I took it all. All! Do you hear me? He'll never rise again. But don't worry. You won't miss anything. I'll drive this sword so deep into your belly it'll make your tonsils wriggle."

The Horla lunged, those huge thigh muscles lifting her off the ground. The sword came streaking through the air and when it met Somelon steel the clang was so loud it shook the tiles off the wall. Allukah's sword shuttered, a blur that shot up her arm, over her pitted shoulder and neck with such force her jaw dropped open. She came down hard, then ran to a far wall to try to recover from the shock.

Sheryl pursued, not rushing but walking casually.

"You killed many men, Allukah. Too many. But you can't kill a Somelon." Sheryl sneered, completely in control, feeling the strength swell in her body as never

160

before. In a quick, silent prayer, she thanked her mother for being who she was, for making Sheryl what she was, so now Sheryl could do this thing.

"Leave here!" Allukah held up an empty hand. There was a thick growth of hair on the palm. "I warn you. Leave now before it's too late."

"It's already too late. For you. It was too late when you and your Horlas came every night to destroy my father's farm. It was too late when you took Kio and my mother's armor." Sheryl choked on the last words. "It was too late when you killed my mother."

"Your mother! You wouldn't know your mother if she sat on your face."

"Thanks to you and your mongrels. But you can't talk your way out of this, Allukah. I've waited too long. Nothing you say can stop me." Sheryl came at her, sword high.

"I warned you. You're too stubborn to listen. You always were." Out of a crouch, Allukah uncoiled, her sword pointed like the spike of a unicorn at the Somelon's stomach.

Sheryl set her feet, prepared for contact. But at the last instant she stepped aside. As Allukah hurled past, Sheryl sliced the blade off her sword.

The momentum of the Horla queen carried her on till she crashed into the far wall. She stuck there with her face smashed flat against the tiles, then slowly slid down to the floor. She was stunned. Blood gushed out of her crushed nose, flowing down to drip off the tips of her breasts.

No. Sheryl wouldn't finish her off. Not like this. Revenge had been slow in its coming and Allukah would have to be fully conscious when her hideous life came to a close. Allukah had to know exactly who it was that cut her ties with this world.

Sheryl kept one of her green eyes on the fat, oily body while the other roamed around the vault looking for water. A gourd would have been perfect, or even a cup, something she could dip in a stagnant pool to splash the vile slime into that bloody face and shake Allukah back to this life before she left it again—for good.

Sheryl was just looking for water. But when she glanced across the sunken body of the corpse lying so stiff and mutilated on the stone table, she looked no further—for there she found the mummified face of her father.

White-hot pokers seemed to pierce her eyes, burning away the image and shriveling Sheryl's brain as if it were a shrimp skewered over an open fire. Sagging, ready to faint, she reached out to steady her melting body. Yet Sheryl was still a Somelon. The shock, sharp and sudden as it was, only lasted for a second. But that second might just as well have been eternity for in it Allukah had the time to shake back her senses, to creep up and swat Sheryl to the ground with her own war club—the one with the Somelon face carved into its head.

The pain left Sheryl's eyes, replaced by the black shroud of oblivion.

Chapter 14

Death of a Somelon

The hut was dark, her bed hard and cold for she'd kicked off the sheets in her sleep. Sheryl heard her father in the next room tapping a scribe across the silver breastplate he'd worked on for as far back as she could remember into her short life. She couldn't see anything except the crack of light beneath the door that kept blinking each time her mother walked past it. Tender hands came to spread Sheryl out on the slippery sheets, a mother's hands. Sheryl could smell her mother's perfume, so soft, sweet, yet tinged with musk. As soon as Sheryl was tucked in, her mother would go out to be with her father. The tapping would stop, the metal would be put aside for tonight, and a new rhythm would begin. And the moaning. Just like in the tunnels.

Sheryl's arms were stretched out above her head. When she tried to pull them back down, they refused to budge. They were stuck.

The door opened, framing her mother's silhouette so tall and slim against the light.

"Mommy?" Sheryl whispered. The silhouette froze, though it gave no answer. Then it started to change.

As if they were balloons, the limbs, the torso, even the head started to swell. A tapered waist sagged into a paunch. Firm arms went flabby, legs as wide as tree trunks. Sheryl blinked, tried to get up. Her hands and feet still wouldn't move. She blinked again, again, and the darkness started to lift. She saw Allukah standing in that doorway.

Consciousness charged back into Sheryl's brain like a horde of stampeding Horlas. She found herself shackled to the same stone table that had held the mummified corpse when first she stepped into this vault. Her head spun, though she thought she saw a green liquid trickling out of Allukah's eyes till she rubbed it away.

"I warned you to go. I owed you that much. But you wouldn't listen to me. You had to have your own way. Pigheaded. Like your father."

In a corner of the vault, the silver armor that her father had made was propped against the tile wall. The face on the breastplate was as scratched and bent as a boxer's, as lumpy as oatmeal, and the golden smile, at least in this light, seemed to have warped into a scowl. On the floor below it were the tools her father had used to create it—the punches, scribes, and the hammer, its blunt nose coated with particles of silver. Allukah must have tried to rework the armor to fit her fat. The clumsy attempts had ruined it.

Other things, however, weren't quite so easy to explain.

An entire wall of the tunnel was lined with shelves that held a collection of items Sheryl recognized immediately. There was a small wooden Pegasus he had fashioned for her with wings of iridescent mother of pearl. Her first bow, presented on her second birthday. Only two feet high and thin enough to fit a baby's hand, its powerful string could drive an arrow clear through an oak plank. And there were snail shell rattles, straw dolls, clay men, and more that only dimly suggested memories. Allukah probably stole them on raids to the farm while Sheryl and her father crouched in the cellar.

"I've hunted for you a long time." Dizzy, Sheryl

couldn't hold her tongue. She shook her head, trying to avoid the needles she swore were piercing her temples. "When I saw you in my mother's armor with your fat. . .I knew one of us had to die."

"My armor!" Allukah screamed so hard the dimple in her chin disappeared and the stubble left on her scalp stood out like an unhusked walnut. The sandpaper rasp was gone from her voice, replaced by a chirping pain she had to keep back, a pain far worse than could be explained by her crushed nose. "I swear I never wanted to kill you. All these years I knew you were after me I avoided a fight. There were many times I could have easily. . .but I let the advantage slip away. Now you've gone too far. I have to choose. Your life or mine. Sheryl, you know what the choice is going to be."

The Horla queen stared blankly as if she were reading the words off the inner surface of her cloudy lenses.

Sheryl felt a cold compress on her face. It was Allukah's clammy paw. She welcomed it for the hand drew some of the tightness out of her scalp. Yet as soon as Allukah felt the responding pressure of her cheek, she pulled away.

"You should have listened, you green-eyed slut." Her mustache bristled like the spine of a black cat. The war club was still clenched in her hand. Sheryl thought of that walnut tree, how it had saved her, given her another few days of life, only to betray her now.

Still naked except for the tight leather belt, Allukah slouched against a wall. The club started to slip out of her fingers. She breathed in long, heavy sighs that whistled through the crushed cartilage of her nose and she popped a couple of the luminous Najucular stones into her mouth. Obviously, she still hadn't recovered from that collision with the wall. The glistening rivulets on her cheeks washed the dried black blood over her chin to spread out into a liquid tatoo over her chest.

The Najucular stones worked quickly. Allukah straightened, shaking the emerald flecks out of her eyes, and in the fog that replaced it, Sheryl could see plans of death drift out of that Horla brain. Allukah wouldn't kill the Somelon quickly. No. Not in an hour, not in one day. It might take a week of suffering before all the hate bloating that fat body could escape, while the soft beauty of Sheryl's body turned into a mushy pulp.

Allukah shuffled toward her again. But something she saw made her stop. It was Kio.

He stood in the entrance to the vault, Sheryl's helmet cradled in his small hands. Somehow he'd found it in the dark, its fragile eagle's wings bent and loose. Somehow he'd wandered through the darkness, stumbling over corpses, following the trail here. He'd done all that, probably expecting it would all be over by the time he got there. But now he saw Allukah standing live, naked, and ugly directly in front of him, and Sheryl spread out on the table exactly the way he'd been back at that other cave. Kio staggered. The helmet dropped, rolled across the floor to the Horla's feet.

"Ah, my little white monkey." Allukah laughed a fat woman's laugh, drawing more strength from Kio's appearance. "Couldn't stay away from me, could you? Think you're man enough to crack my thighs again? Or did you just come to watch?"

His eyes followed the sweep of her hand to the stone table and the way they pulsed, he might have seen himself chained there instead of the Somelon.

"Of course you've come to watch. That's all you can do."

Kio started to shrink, as though he were a plant drawing in its vines that were too far extended, too vulnerable. He took a step backward.

"Don't go. Don't leave us. The fun's just begun." Allukah glanced to Sheryl, watching the hope raised by Kio's entrance flicker and die. Then she pounced on him and dragged him over to the table.

"She was waiting for you. See the welcome in her face? Isn't it queer? She saved others. Why can't she save herself?" Allukah shook him as easily as if he were a rabbit caught by the ears before throwing him aside. Kio crawled to a corner to hide his head in his hands.

"You really didn't expect him to save you." Allukah leaned low, breathing her foul, goatish breath directly into Sheryl's face. "I'm disappointed in you. That's really scraping the bottom of the old wine barrel. There isn't an ounce of courage left in his puny little body. He'll stand by to watch you die, even help me if I order him to. But I don't want his help. This job I'll do all by myself. It cries out for the personal touch. Every twinge, every twist of agony will come out of my hand. And when I'm done, all I have to do is whistle. He'll come running to place his neck on the blade of my sword, beg me to slit his throat. That's the kind of man you picked. For a Somelon, you're not very bright. You make me ashamed."

Allukah snarled at Kio. Letting out a weak cry, he cowered deeper into his corner. Like a dog whipped too often, his response was conditioned by abuse. He'd become so self-conscious that he feared the simplest action, even breathing, might earn him another beating. Allukah had that power to turn men into animals, though not lions or eagles, but jackasses and sheep.

Turning her back on him, she walked to the far side of the cave where slots and pigeonholes were cut into the walls.

"I've dreamed of this day ever since you started your plot to steal him away from me. I should have known

167

you couldn't be trusted the first time your head peeked up between my legs. But I was a fool and you took advantage of that. Well, I'm a fool no more.''

Sheryl lay still and quiet on the stone table. The physical confusion had finally left her mind, only to make more than enough room for the emotional turmoil to scramble in. Allukah. The sword. Her father's corpse. The single slice that cut him in two pieces. Then Allukah again. Sheryl looked at the ogre's wide, bare back dotted with hair. Those were powerful muscles, thought not nearly powerful enough to stop the Somelon if she were free. When Sheryl tugged at the manacles holding her hands and feet, it was only a reflex action. She didn't expect it to do any good. And it didn't. All it did was make Allukah turn around.

''Pull all you want, Somelon. Those chains were forged from invar by the magician Praxus to hold the Horla twins. They can't be broken. I wish your father had used them on you before you spoiled.''

Her father! Sheryl had desecrated his poor dead body. Maybe it wasn't her fault that the body was here, but that didn't change what she'd done. Allukah must have stolen it from the caravan that was carrying it home, taken it when she found out who it was, who it belonged to. Only a demon could have done those perverted things to his corpse. And only Sheryl could have mutilated it the way she had. If only she'd known! Then she wouldn't be lying here now, helpless. She wouldn't have given Allukah those few seconds she needed to knock her out. If only she'd known! But a Somelon is supposed to know everything. She couldn't afford not to. And for her punishment, she would have to bear the brunt of Allukah's madness.

The pain wouldn't bother her. No matter what travesty the Horla witch practiced on her body, Sheryl wouldn't even flinch. That was the Somelon way, even though that indifference to pain would almost certainly inspire Allukah to new, unsurpassed heights of cruelty. Sheryl knew all that, so it flipped through her mind easily, without much effect. None of it mattered.

What did matter was that the three bodies—Kio's, Sheryl's, and her father's—would be left to rot in this lightless dungeon along with Allukah's pets. A warrior's body should be placed under the ground where the roots of trees and plants can reach it, where it can mix with the soil to be pumped back into the light through a tangled botanical network of capillaries and cells to live again, beginning the cycle of life at the bottom of the chain, through animals and men, till it became a warrior again. That's how her father should rest, in the tips of rose petals, in the rustling leaves of an elm. He shouldn't be piled up with the rest with the sweat and slime of the Horla bitch still clinging to him.

And Kio. Poor, dear Kio. Sheryl couldn't raise her head high enough off the stone slab to see where he was, though his whimpering was loud enough to hear as he sang his sad tale of woe to the concrete floor, reliving every humiliating detail of his captivity in the Jibway caves. It is better that he came here. Stripped of his manhood and pride, he wouldn't survive very long without her protection. If only he didn't have to endure the long ordeal of her dying that was about to begin. Too bad he couldn't die first. Knowing he was there all the while it happened would be the single thing capable of piercing through her tough, Somelon facade.

Allukah rummaged through her trophy shelves flinging talismans, luminous Najucular stones, scalps and dried male members into the air, cursing, shattering vases and icons, till finally she found what she was searching for.

"Here it is!" She cried with a gaseous bubble of enthusiasm. "I had this made for me as soon as I joined the Horlas. I knew it'd come in handy some day. And this is the day."

Turning around, she held it out into the torchlight. It was a brass billet, two feet long by three inches in diameter. All along its length, spikes stuck out at sharp angles, then curved back toward the handle. At the tip was a gleaming, barbed hook. This tool would slide in between folds of flesh easily enough. But when it was pulled out, the hook and spikes would dig deep, tearing and shredding like the jaws of some fabulous shark. Shining now in the flickering light, the wand was almost beautiful in its stark, brutal function. It was a glowing candle of death.

"A fascinating tool. As breathtaking as your Somelon beauty." Light on her feet, an eager Allukah swept toward Sheryl without removing her eyes from the shaft. "As beautiful as I am ugly. A fitting way to bring your thieving life to an end. When I'm done, even your Kio won't be able to look at you without throwing up his guts. This is my justice. Horla justice. To destroy your beauty as you destroyed mine."

In her other paw, Allukah held a dagger and she used it to cut away the straps holding Sheryl's breastplate in place. Lifting the armor like the cover off a roast pheasant, she tore away the thin chemise that lay beneath.

"My God," Allukah gasped, holding onto the table for support. Your beauty is almost painful. Even when I saw it back at the Great Hut, I might not have believed it was possible if I hadn't once been even more beautiful. That was before you came to rob me. That was before you came, and I went ugly. Before you had the gall to be born."

Allukah ran the tool through Sheryl's hair, combing it out with the spikes.

"Long ago, I had golden hair too. Shamask rose every morning just to see me. Once the moon grew so jealous it chased after the sun and stood between us, plunging the whole world into darkness. That's how magnificent I was."

Her horny paw rose up to what remained of her scalp and pulled out a few strands of kinky black strands, then flung them aside in disgust.

The tool moved down to Sheryl's cheek, grazing the creamy skin. She felt nothing but the cold metal drawing the heat out of her body, then the trickle of blood from tiny cuts.

"Once men butchered each other for a glimpse of my face, knowing all the while I was beyond their reach."

The wand drifted along, scratching her breasts as deep as a cat's claw.

"My breasts were fuller than yours. And firmer, sticking straight out of my chest. My nipples were as hard as your finger so I had to keep them pressed flat by my armor or drive all men wild."

Biting with the sting of swarming mosquitoes, the brass billet glided over her stomach, pausing at the navel. When it touched that spot, Sheryl drew a quick breath despite herself.

With a bent finger, Allukah scooped up the small drops that came oozing out. Raising it to her mouth, she licked away the blood.

"Your blood is my blood. We're one body. The same egg. Yet men run to your beauty and away from my deformity. But once you're dead, all that beauty will return to me, back to its source. I'll be a caterpillar turning into a butterfly. Can't you see it? Me, Allukah, queen of the Horlas, a fragile butterfly perched on the

171

edge of a daffodil?''

She laughed and the wand soared to Sheryl's thighs which were held open by the chains.

"This is the reason I fell. I kept my legs crossed to the gods, but opened them for a mere man, so they punished me. That's when the gods sent you to turn my teeth from pearls to coal, to squash my nose, swell out my belly, turn my muscles to fat. You took it all from me and kept it for yourself. But now I get it back. I'll send this wand inside you and let you feel the fire I felt when you were born.''

The rod went as far as her knees before it changed direction and aimed for the place the legs came together in a golden triangle. It stopped just before the hook bit.

"Slowly, Sheryl. Very slowly. One minute for each of the years I spent in hell with the Horlas. Then I'll split you open from one end to the next, starting at the place you began to work your evil against me.''

The wand shot up to Sheryl's thighs again, changing direction at the last instant.

"My beauty!''

The wand flew up, then down this time taking a small piece of the Somelon's most precious flesh.

"My life!''

Allukah's huge arm pumped back and forth, then held, bicep bulging.

"With this thrust I get it all back!''

Sheryl braced herself. Allukah's mouth tightened, holding the breath for the plunge. Then, with a loud pop, her head split open. The queen of the Horlas crumpled to the floor.

Kio stood over her, the silver-flecked hammer of Sheryl's father clenched tight in his hand. His whole face was brilliant with wonder over what he had done and how he had managed to do it. The agony of every atrocity that had been worked on him concentrated itself in the nose of the mallet and when Allukah grabbed desperately to press her lips to Sheryl's foot, the hammer came down again. Then again. Muscles that knew how to pulverize granite, blows that once turned marble into dust rained down on the hollow skull as the artist took his revenge on life, resculpting the world till Allukah's brains leaked out onto the concrete and mixed with the stagnant water. Kio beat down the queen of the Horlas, not stopping till the only motion left in her fat body was the quiver of dead muscles.

"Those eyes. Those impenetrable eyes!" Kio yelled, reaching for her dagger. Wrestling Allukah's head between his knees, he sliced away the layer of opaque skin that hid her eyes.

"Sheryl!" He called, letting the flaccid body flounce back to the floor. "They're green. Allukah's eyes are green. Like yours. Like a Somelon's."

"Green eyes," she murmured. "Like my mother's."

The cold concrete sapped the warmth out of the mountain of flesh that had been the queen of the Horlas. She lay there sagging like a beached whale. But beneath her left breast, you could still make out the six-pointed star—the place where Cupid's arrow had struck her when she met Sheryl's father so many years ago.

Sheryl was running. Her feet and hands were bound by the unbreakable chains of Praxus, yet she ran in her mind, away from this terrible place, away from her father's corpse, away from Allukah. Her lungs gulped for air, she thrashed wildly. Her head flipped from side to side and all she saw was the wolfish smile of Maskim repeating over and over.

"You may kill Allukah, but her daughter will stalk

173

you from that day on. You can't win a battle against Allukah's daughter anymore than you can catch your reflection in a mirror."

Maskim stayed hot on her heels, riding atop a Somelon's shoulders. That Somelon was Sheryl. She was chasing herself.

Powerless, Kio watched her. He heard her cries and for the first time he saw not a warrior, but a woman, naked and vulnerable. Somehow that sight drove the selfish anxiety out of his head. He felt the strength returning, surging through his arms, his legs, bulging out through his thighs.

Sheryl was falling into the same pit that had held him a prisoner since the caravan, a choking, bottomless shaft of self pity. He wasn't going to stand by and let it happen. No, she'd taught him that much. Nobody should run away from living. He'd force her to turn around and being only a man, he knew only one way to do that.

The brass wand filled his eye. Stooping, he tore it from Allukah's stiffening grip. Kio looked at the places where the wand touched Sheryl, the swelling cuts of her cheeks, her breasts, stomach, her thighs. Drawing back the wand, he flung it against the wall with such force it shattered in a rain of metal and tile.

"Kio," Sheryl moaned, licking her lips.

He couldn't waste another minute. Tearing off the blue robe, he draped it over Allukah's head, cutting off the glow of those green eyes. Thick with sweat and oil, his skin shone in the torchlight, and through the liquid veil of tears hanging over her, Sheryl imagined for a moment that he had three legs.

"Kio. I thought—"

"I know what you thought." Kio glanced down at himself with undeniable pride. "It's what I wanted you to think because I thought I hated you. You were too much a woman for any one man. The Horlas only wanted my ear, but Allukah castrated my mind. I didn't think I'd ever feel again, that I'd ever be able to. . . well, now I know I will. I have to."

And he did. Climbing on to the table, he covered her nakedness with his own. Sheryl strained against the chains, not so much to be free as to meet his flesh sliding inside her. Their eyes locked, cascading into each other from opposite ends of eternity. One chain snapped. then another. Her arms folded over him. Her legs curled around his waist. And once and for all, he showed her how much man was still left inside him.

Chapter 15

Healing

She couldn't help him. She hadn't the strength and he'd made her so sore she couldn't even sit. So Sheryl lay back on the table with the chains of Praxus dripping from her wrists and ankles, waiting for him to finish.

Kio found her father's body in a small room lined with stalls and white porcelain bowls, exactly where Allukah had hidden it. Lugging the stiff corpse ripe with embalming fluid all the way out to the light, he scooped a hole in a soft heap of rubble with his bare hands and placed the dead man inside. Kio was particularly careful to bring the mummy's severed penis along too. He knew what it felt like to be half a man, even if he didn't know what it felt like to be dead.

Next, though the work knotted his stomach, he wrestled the bloated body of the Horla queen up through the entrance and placed the battered silver armor on her chest before burying her in the grave close to her husband. The Somelon war club served as the marker, the same one Sheryl had carved from the walnut's branch.

Once these chores were out of the way, Kio washed himself in the cold water running out of the cracks in the tiled walls. He took out his robe, the one with the green and red stripes, the one Sheryl had given him. As soon as the dyed silk slid over his skin, a hairy leg poked through the slit. Though he might have blushed unconsciously, Kio no longer fought the feeling. He was glad to feel anything again, and there was no strength to spare. Someone had to take care of Sheryl.

"It's time for us to leave this place."

Rolling her head on the stone slab, she looked at Kio as though he spoke in some foreign language. She waited for him to take her hand, and only then swung around to drop her bare feet on the concrete. While Kio dressed her, her limp hands wandered along the shelves, finally coming to rest on the wooden Pegasus with the clam-shell wings.

"She told me she rode this horse down from Somelon," Sheryl twisted the statue in her hands, talking to no one in particular. "I knew Kryl carved it. But I believed her anyway."

"Leave it here, Sheryl." He unfolded her fingers from around the carving. "Leave it here with everything else."

All her weight leaned down on his shoulders as he lead her out through the tunnels, yet she still held on to the figurine, clutching it to her steel breast. They passed the rows of dead corpses, the ghost wagons with their skeleton crews, then, squeezing through the bars, they mounted the stairs. Kio coached her every step and she obeyed without making a sound until the sunlight rushed into her wide-open irises. Then she crumbled, pulling Kio down with her.

Shamask smiled. There was no way he could tell what had happened in the tunnels beneath the Anhatan mounds. It didn't matter. He would have his revenge now that the Somelon had no strength left to resist him.

"It's no use, Kio. I can't go any further. Leave me here—with my parents." As she lay on the grave, her head hung down like a drunk's with the knotted ropes of hair covering her face. The cuts on her white thighs and cheeks had turned a deep purple. And still she held on to the wooden statue, the wings pearl-white in the morning sunlight.

Kio did leave her there, though only long enough to find the stallion and lead it carefully back over the mounds. The pony didn't follow. She knew the stallion was coming back.

Stripping the handrails from the tunnel entrance and lashing them to her breastplate, Kio fashioned a litter to tie to the stallion. Green plastic bags dug out of the rubble were stuffed with rolls of microfilm and the tattered pages of books for cushions. Once she lay secure on the pallet, Kio knocked the stones out from under the granite block. It crashed down, sealing the mouth of the tomb for what he hoped would be forever.

The trip back over the mounds was long and tortuous. Every step of the horse's hooves had to be placed by hand, the beast whipped up one slope, then reined down the next. But Kio savored every sweating minute of it, flattering himself now that she was helpless and so dependent on him. Like a monk ending a long fast, Kio glutted himself with pride.

Through it all, Sheryl slumped silently, bouncing from one rock to another, her past crowded so tightly in her brain that only one memory at a time could leak out to relieve some of the pressure.

On the bank of the Tent River, it was soon clear that they couldn't swim the currents as they had on the way here—not with Sheryl the way she was. Kio stood watching the gray waters roll, trying to think where he could find something to lash together for a raft, when the pony snuck up and bit him on the elbow. Kio slapped at her, but the animal was too quick. She trotted away, peeking back over her shoulder, neighing at him as only a Horla pony could do. He decided he couldn't let the animal get away that easily. She had to be taught a lesson before she got completely out of hand and refused to carry a rider. So he started chasing her. The pony ran a few yards ahead of him, slowing when he slowed, racing every time he tried to close ground, until they ran into a small valley. Only then did the pony let Kio catch up.

When he raised a hand to slap her nose, the pony knocked him so hard Kio spun completely around. And there, before him, gaped the entrance to another tunnel, one that led beneath the river. Turning back to the pony, he cuffed her ear, though the blow was playful, almost a pet, and the animal knelt down to let him climb on her back. They rode back for Sheryl and the stallion.

After the tunnel, there were the palisades to climb, and the animals took eagerly to the rocky crags, pawing with their hooves, pulling in long, prancing strides. On the summit, Kio stopped long enough to look back over the Tent River. The Anhatan mounds were haunted by ghosts of every type and shape. One of those ghosts had been his own spirit, the one Allukah stripped from his flesh. Now he had it back. For good. The two hemispheres of his personality reunited, cemented with the blood of the Horla queen. Her soul, and the soul of her husband, would go unnoticed among the eight million or so others already there.

Sheryl. She looked so tiny sitting in the litter, her green eyes as deep, as dark as the eyes of the little Horla woman who met Kio when he entered the camp, who washed his face only to die despite her compassion. But Sheryl was not going to die. He'd see to that. Kio had enough strength to share with her, enough to take her suffering as his own. Every time the litter hit a bump, she winced as though it were the war club pounding her skull. Kio winced along with her. No matter how strong a Somelon was built, she too had a keystone. Remove it, and the facade crumbled. It was Kio's challenge to rebuild, put the stones back together again. And in doing that, he had the chance to leave a few out, or put some new ones in. When he was done, she'd be stronger. So would he from the work of it. It would take a great man to strangle the memory of Allukah. Kio was confident that he was that man.

Moving away from the river, Kio paused at the Roc's nest long enough to find a giant feather to drape over Sheryl to keep her warm while at the same time protect her from that jealous sun. The sight of what he did made Shamask cringe and he cursed the small man from that point on.

Round the table of the Colossi, the seats were all taken. Propped on their elbows, the titans feasted while the food steamed up out of the bowls, forming clouds that drifted away to drizzle over the two returning pilgrims. The Roc feather kept Sheryl dry.

Once they left the open plain, Sheryl fell asleep so she never saw the way the centaurs swarmed out of the bushes. Surrounding the stallion, they refused to let Kio pass until they assured themselves that he meant her no harm.

"Allukah?" The largest of them asked Kio, running his double-thumbed hand through a thick beard. His chest was bare, his four-legged part speckled as a roan.

Kio told them of Allukah and the rest of the centaurs shook their heads sadly.

"We always knew it would come to this. It's better the ordeal is over."

Though they escorted the couple through the forest, it was mostly a formality since it would be months before the Horlas could regroup under their new master, Amurti. And there was no question that they would regroup. Still, it made the centaurs happy to think they were serving a Somelon, so Kio said nothing.

The silent cortege moved along without incident till they came in sight of the lava beds. Then a murmur spread through the centaurs. Hooves broke rhythm, their steps halting, erratic, for they found fresh springs bubbling through the holes left by the bodies of the ancient nymphs and the stream ran crystal and fast with white water once again. Noses twitching, the centaurs struggled mightily with their instincts when they saw the new nymphs break the water, their miniature bodies darting through the foam. And when the nymphs saw the centaurs, they skirted coyly along the banks, chattering like chipmunks, for they knew how weak these man-beasts really were, and they were delighted to tease them. The centaurs wrestled their eyes toward heaven, shivering, but none of them broke out of line.

"What's the matter?" Kio kidded them. "Don't centaurs like women?" For his trouble, Kio earned only dirty looks as the centaurs ground their teeth, sighing in heavy breaths.

The nymphs started singing songs that drove men wild and when the centaurs finally turned to cross the stream, they playfully snatched at their hooves. The centaurs showed no sign that they knew the nymphs were there, though they broke into a gallop and raced across to the opposite shore. Centaurs were strong, but they didn't think they were that strong.

Upstream a mermaid sat sunning herself, watching it all with some amusement. Spying Kio, she raised herself on one elbow and waved to him. Kio returned the wave as she slipped into the water, disappearing with a hard slap of her tail that splashed a few drops on Sheryl's face, waking her.

"What was that?" Sheryl cried, searching absently

for her sword.

"An otter, Sheryl. Only an otter." He told her, sure she didn't really want to know about the mermaid. She settled back, shifting the carved Pegasus to a cradle beneath her chin.

At the rim of the Sugar Desert, the centaurs stepped aside, waiting for Kio to catch up with them.

"We can go no further," the large, speckled centaur told him, his voice trembling each time his eyes drifted back along the trail in the direction of the lava beds. "The desert sand works its way between the clefts of our hooves and makes us lame. But you'll be all right from here to Centropolis."

"Then let me thank you for bringing us this far."

"It is our privilege. You'll take care of her?" The centaur looked away, for already a few of the others had begun circling back.

"None could do better."

Kneeling at Sheryl's side, the centaur waited for a sign. When she lay there without moving, Kio took her hand and placed it on the woolly head. The centaur kissed her palm, then he was off, dissolving into the brush as quickly as he came.

Already the desert had started to cool as Shamask settled beyond the ring of Jibway mountains and Kio let the stallion walk loose to find his own way through the dark. To make the time go smoother, and to soothe Sheryl, Kio sang an old, rambling song about the sea that his grandmother had taught him. Night animals wriggled out of their burrows to fill the black velvet with diamond eyes and some of them, particularly the coyotes, answered his song with a few lines of their own.

"Here!" Sheryl's cry broke through his resonant tenor. She threw off the Roc feather.

Kio looked around. He saw nothing except the

dancing eyes of the animals and a few glowing Najucular stones.

"Take my sword, Kio. Tap it on the ground." She held the weapon out, shaking in her hands. "Hurry, Kio. Please."

He obeyed, not because he expected anything to come of it, but to humor her, not wanting to stir her up. So he took the sword, drove the shining blade into the sand.

Off to her right, a scraggly weed began to twitch like a hairy mole on a giant's face. The plant tumbled and out of its roots slithered a dust-coated creature with red eyes. Kio jumped back, straining to swing the broad sword over his head to defend Sheryl.

"Put down the sword, Kio. Kryl is my friend—my dearest, oldest friend."

Kryl slid over the sand to her side, keeping Kio in front of him all the way.

"Allukah's dead. Isn't she?" Kryl chewed the words. There was no welcome, only resignation in his dry voice.

"Yes." Sheryl was glad her face was hidden in the darkness.

"Do you know who you killed?" The old man pulled himself on to the litter. Skittish, the stallion's hooves tore at the sand though he stayed where he was.

"I know." Kio pushed the old man off the litter and stood between them. "I killed her, you old cripple. I did!"

"Cripple?" Kryl floundered in the dust, snorting. "Well, I guess your eyes are sharper than your brain. Come on. Get some wood. No sense sitting around in the dark like a bunch of criminals."

The young man let the old man crawl around doing most of the work, dragging branches and small logs. Kio stalled as long as he could, maybe picking up a twig to add to the slowly growing pile, because he didn't like the tone of Kryl's voice. The old man hadn't enough respect for Sheryl, especially after all she'd been through. He treated her with too much familiarity. And there was something else too, something that made jealousy crawl around inside him.

When he decided the pile was big enough, Kio took some of the stuffing out of the green plastic pillows he'd made for Sheryl, sprinkling scraps of microfilm and crumbled paper pages of indecipherable books over the wood. Digging deep into the bag, his hand came out with a cracked leather book cover, its spine long fractured. That he threw over his shoulder into the night where a jackal scurried out to catch it. But the skin had lost its taste years ago and the jackal coughed it back out on the ground, leaving the gilded letters, *The Decline and Fall of the Roman Empire,* covered with a thick slime.

"Maybe the ancient ones didn't know how to get along with one another," Kio snickered, taking fire out of Sheryl's bag. "But they sure knew how to make kindling."

While the young man was busy, Kryl squirmed over to the litter once more. He took Sheryl's hand and tugged it, hard. The wooden figurine fell into the dirt. She scrambled after it, retrieved it, then dusted it off with a bit too much care.

"Get over by the fire," he told her. "You've sulked long enough. It's time to talk."

"Leave her alone," Kio jumped to his feet.

Kryl ignored the warning and Sheryl left the litter to take a place by the fire.

"I've no meat for you today, Kryl." Her voice was weak, almost a whisper.

"It's a bad night for eating."

"I'll go get something to fill your stomach, Sheryl."

Kio started to go, but she grabbed him, pulled him down to sit by her side.

"No, Kio. Stay with me." She looked deep into his eyes, her lids fluttering. Then suddenly she turned away to Kryl.

"Why didn't you tell me?"

"Because everybody knew. Everybody," the old teeth clicked defensively. "Everybody but you, Sheryl. And that was only because you didn't want to know."

"But Allukah. How could my father ever have. . . and she. . .well, my mother was gentle, warm, the most beautiful Somelon who ever walked the earth. What happened?"

She wasn't looking at the old man now, or at Kio either. She might have asked the question of the night. It answered with a jackal's giggle.

"Maybe it isn't true, Sheryl." Kio held her, tried to comfort her, but even he didn't believe what he said.

"It's true," the old man muttered.

"How do you know? Who the hell are you, anyway? Some legless snake that digs into the ground? Some dirty. . ."

"I wasn't always this way. Sheryl will tell you. But that's not important anymore." Kryl took a deep breath like a man about to lift a heavy weight.

"Sheryl. Do you remember what I told you the last time we were together. About the Somelon, the one who gave up her command on Mount Palus?"

"Yes. The parable. Why must old men insist on speaking in parables, or idiotic riddles like Maskim? Why can't you just come out and tell me, Kryl?"

"Listen to me, girl!" Kryl buried his fist in the dirt.

Kio didn't like what was happening. Not one bit. He was ready to go after the legless worm, but Sheryl held him back, digging her fingers into his arm.

185

"I did tell you. Your mother gave up too much for your father, and what she gave up, she had no right to give. She turned her back on her own people, left a Somelon's world to become a wife, then a mother. Once it was done, there was no way to go back, to put the pieces together the way they were. So your father became everything, and no man can possibly fill a need that great. She clung to him like a wet leaf, convinced she'd done the right thing. And at first it looked like things might really work out. Their love was strong enough to hide the doubts. For a while."

Kryl patted the sand, smoothing over the hole his fist had dug.

"The first cracks appeared when your mother saw the old women begging in the streets, the hags and dried-up whores who'd lost everything when their feminine charms deserted them. It made her wonder. She started examining herself everyday for signs of age. We laughed at her, your father and I, and we kidded her. She was always trying a new cream, lotion, or potion to preserve and protect her skin. Maybe we were cruel. But if you saw the way she looked then, you'd understand. Her beauty was so intense, like gold, staying gold no matter what you'd do to it, never tarnishing, never losing its gleam."

Secretly, Kio tried to catch Sheryl's eye. He failed for the only thing the Somelon saw now were the images thick on the old man's voice.

"She was a woman compelled and when you began to swell her belly, she confided to me how ugly and fat it made her feel. Ashamed to let your father see her, she wore loose, ill-fitting robes, shrank back everytime he tried to touch her. It was a warning, a cry for help neither he nor I recognized. And after you were born, I noticed the way her eyes always melted when your father played with you. It was jealousy. The same kind of jealousy simmering now in this man of yours."

Kryl flicked his head at Kio, without looking up from the sand.

"Jealous?" The young man stammered. "Of what? A cripple? Maybe he is your friend, Sheryl. But I'd like to teach him a lesson."

She pulled him back down again, sharply.

"Just listen to him, Kio. We have to know everything and Kryl's the only one who'd dare tell us."

"Yes," the old man rocked back, tottering on his stumps like a hunter caught in quicksand. "Listen to me, you young duck and maybe you'll see some of yourself in Allukah. Yes, she was jealous, though she was strong enough to hide that too until your hair grew long and silky, till the child turned into a tiny woman. Then your father's attention to you became adulterous. Every kiss he gave you was stolen from her."

"That isn't enough to change anybody into a monster," Kio fidgeted.

"Isn't it? Well, Allukah wasn't just anybody. Not by a long shot. She was a goddess who threw it up in the faces of the gods for a weak, mortal, flesh and blood man. Now she saw herself getting older, losing the only thing she had left that made her unique. She saw you taking away her husband. Then what would she have but the gutter to look forward to? When you put your arm around her she felt cold. When you went to your father her cheeks burned. It all came to a head that night after she put you to sleep. There in their bedroom, she had your father fully, unconditionally. They were one flesh, moving with one motion, man and woman. Then you walked in on them. From shame your father covered himself and rushed to your side. While he tried to soothe you with soft words and hugs, carrying you in his arms back to your room, your mother lay alone, shaking, afraid. That's when Allukah was born—out of spite."

"In the tunnel! That's why she cried out when I found her there, bouncing like. . .yet I can't even remember it happening the way you say it did." Her face contorted as she strained to make some sense out of all this. "I can't believe it, Kryl. My mother was blonde, slim, beautiful. As beautiful as—"

"As you are, Sheryl?" Sifting through the dirt, Kryl found a luminous Najucular stone. He held it out to her.

"Envy started the erosion. This did the rest. The cold fire imprisoned in these stones is a small piece of the Great Mushroom War, of the fire that blasted the Sugar Desert into the face of the world. Those old harpies, the blue Boroka women, came to your mother swearing these rocks had magical powers. They had power—the power to destroy. Allukah took them to preserve her beauty. Instead they turned her into a deformed freak."

He flung the stone out into the night. Taking it for a firefly, a toad hopped up and swallowed it before it hit the ground.

"The bed was empty when your father returned from your room. He came to me. Crying, he told me everything. I warned him to leave that place right away, to take you to Centropolis. But no, he expected her to come back home to her husband, her baby. He'd wait. It was only a matter of time and when she came back he'd welcome her without a word of reproach. The fool!" Kryl cried, his throat so dry the last words came out in a trill. "Oh, she came back, all right. But when she did she was riding at the head of a band of Horlas."

"Why, Kryl? Why the Horlas? Did she want to kill us?"

"Maybe. That would have been one kind of revenge. But maybe she wanted your father to know where she was, too, as if to say, 'you thought I was ugly. To the Horlas it doesn't matter.' The Horlas bred madness into the human race, so with them her fantasies were true until the Najucular stones turned even her ugliness into reality, justifying everything she'd done. Yet remember, Sheryl. When Allukah came to raid your little farm, she knew where you and your father were hiding. She could have destroyed you both any time she wanted, burned the hut with you in it. She never did." Kryl's voice petered out. "Of course, she might also have come back for her silver armor."

"Well, she got that back," Sheryl croaked. "And my father, too. Now you're telling me it's all my fault—the whole terrible thing."

"Your fault?" Puzzled, Kio squeezed his forehead into a prune, then turned on Kryl.

"Are you blaming her? If you think for one second that I'm going to sit by while you—"

"Don't be a fool."

"I'm not. I'm being cold and logical," she insisted, though emotion threaded through her voice. "If it wasn't for me, mother and father would have had a happy life together. They'd have. . ."

"Now you're talking like Allukah. What's wrong with you, anyway? Are you trying to think your way into hell the way she did? Look, Sheryl. Allukah was a warrior. She was born to fight, not to love. She was strong and even if she'd give up a castle in the clouds for a hut in a cow-pied pasture, she could have handled it—if it wasn't for the Najucular stones. If you need to blame something, blame them. And if you weren't there, what would have happend to your father, alone? Because of you he had a happy life in spite of everything. You were all that was good in your mother. He loved you for it. It made his life a success.''

"Okay. Enough of this." Kio kicked at the desert sand. "They're dead now. Good or bad. Happy or sad. They had their chance. They're dead. We're alive. The two of us. It's our turn. We'll make some mistakes. But that's all right too. Leave it behind, Sheryl. Let them go to wherever people like that go.''

"I hate to admit it. Yet the little clown's right, Sheryl.''

Through the slits of his lids, Kryl watched Kio take her in his arms. She melted as quickly as wax in front of the fire. It wasn't a sight that pleased the old man. She was a Somelon, and no Somelon should be tied down to a man. Still, she hadn't given anything up for Kio. She'd taken him freely, without paying a price, and that might make all the difference.

Kio peeled her white hands off the wooden Pegasus and threw it back into the fire. The flames flared up for a second, then settled back down.

"Now that we've had a grand old time raking ourselves over the coals, I'm going to get us something to eat.''

He pulled her away from the fire and forced her to lay down. Then he turned his back on her.

"He's kinda small, you know?" Kryl observed as Kio disappeared into the darkness.

"Only on the outside.''

Kryl's hands left the sand to massage the tips of the stumps that once were his legs.

"She did that to you, didn't she?" Sheryl searched through the orange flames with her green eyes without finding a sign that the winged statue of the horse ever existed.

"These? Yes. To this day I'm not sure whether she

did it out of hate. . .or love. She saved my life that day. The rest of her Horlas wanted to slit my throat and fill it with sand. But she persuaded them that it would be more fun to leave me here alone, in the middle of the desert without any legs. I don't know. Maybe she didn't even recognize me. I'll never know."

"Tomorrow you'll go with us." She came around the fire to take his peeling hands into her own.

"No." The old man squirmed uncomfortable from years of being alone. "The desert is my home. I know it as well as it knows me. Anyway, this is the time for you to be alone. With him."

"Don't worry about Kio. We won't go off the deep end if you come walking into our bedroom and surprise us some night."

"You don't need me hanging around like a slug."

"No. You're right there," Kio called, stepping out of the night with a brace of quail hanging from either hand. "But you need us."

In the morning, after they scattered the ashes of the cold fire, they rode out with Kryl filling the litter. Kio's pony pressed close to the stallion.

"You know, Kio." Sheryl leaned over to whisper. "You're taking a big chance with me. They say that if you want to see what your wife will look like when she grows old, to look at her mother."

The idea stopped Kio for a second. He pulled rein, letting the pony fall behind. Then he came riding back to catch up to the stallion.

"I guess that's a chance I'll have to take," he smiled. "Anyway, you might be taking a bigger chance. After all, you've never even met my father."